The Poetry Cafe

by

John Newlin

Also by Casa de Snapdragon

A Scattering of Imperfections
Katrina K Guarascio

Harriet Murphy – A Little Bit of Something
Janet k. Brennan

I Found My Father in a Women's Prison
Dr. Tracey Brown

A Dance in the Woods
Janet K. Brennan

Recollections of an Old Mind, West
Janet K. Brennan

Visit https://www.casadesnapdragon.com for details on these books and others.

The Poetry Cafe

John Newlin

Published by Casa de Snapdragon Publishing Company

Copyright 2009, John Newlin. All rights reserved.

All rights reserved. No portion of this publication may be reproduced, stored in a retrieval system, or transmitted in any form or by any means, electronic, mechanical, photocopying, recording, or otherwise without the prior written permission of John Newlin unless such copying is expressly permitted by federal copyright law. Address inquiries to Permissions, Casa de Snapdragon, 12901 Bryce Court NE, Albuquerque, NM 87112.

Library of Congress Control Number: 2009921217
ISBN: 978-0-9840530-1-8

Published by
Casa de Snapdragon Publishing Company
12901 Bryce Avenue, NE
Albuquerque, NM 87112
http://www.casadesnapdragon.com

Cover painting "Starry Night Over the Rhône" by Vincent Van Gogh.

Printed in the United States of America

Beyond the Pale

I hear the sound of laughter,
distant music upon my ear,
far away I can see their fires
dancing in the sky's dark mirror.

The desert is cold in the dry night,
yon ocean is briny and gray,
the forest is thick and lonely,
the mountains so very far away.

In the village there is dancing,
glad music and warmth and jest,
soft voices echo in the night
as the loved speak with the blessed.

I feel their distant melodies
and sway slowly in the gloom;
dancing a dance long forgotten
with a ghostly partner exhumed.

There is a gate in the distance,
at the end of the dwindling trail.
I cannot go there this raw night;
I must abide beyond the pale.

Judith Anne

Her hair hangs down - a chestnut frame -
round a portrait face shining through;
liquid eyes clad in russet brown
gleaming In the sun like morning dew.

I knew her once, and was beguiled
by her beauty and her winsome way,
her gentleness came down hard upon me
and held me captive in Its sway.

But my eyes then had not ripened
and my ears missed her subtle beat;
I was all ablaze with manly youth,
giving out less light than heat.

I yearned to know her untapped well
and to draw passion's first deep drink;
her thirst, as keen as was mine
spurred me, but stayed me at the brink.

She took not a footstep beyond
my arrogance—my blinding pride
with honest ardor unrequited
the once and future chance died.

The chance expired, but not the flame
that burned in memory's prison;
then time and circumstance contrived
to fan the flame and singe honor's vision.

Her dark eyes melted down my soul
to where it longed to be
and left me in painful splendor
under tearful skies by the sea,

Now gold grains are swiftly falling
through the narrow neck of glass,
and each moment that I'm without her
is all the pain that shall come to pass.

Sun, Moon, and Stars

Lambent astral luminance is reflected
in twin orbs
of gray, green, blue
and finally brown
dilating in hypnotic awe
of stellar passion,
unleashed across the obscure darkness
wrenching the satellite from orbit,
threatening apogean escape.

Tremors undulate
through the whirling sphere
while celestial eyes
bleed diamond drops,
shimmering tears in silent sorrow,
spangling the Stygian void.

The axis leans,
the balance sways,
descent through ether space
is hastened by denial,
but not beyond the afterglow
of luminary brilliance.

Bewitched sphere,
divided by merciless terminator
into ebon and blazing discs
revolves in measured rhythm,
capturing and absorbing
sunburst energy cascading
from distant solar fountain.

Incandescent splendor tempts
the whirling body;
lava red desire
bursts from the core;
swollen monoliths rise and fall
in reverent communion
with life giving, soul searing radiance.

Zenith approaches, overwhelms
and unsated sphere defies cosmic law,
soars upward, unheeding,
in source brightness.
Until, spent and charred,
is recaptured and spins away
shrouded in misty lament,
for the shattered Icarean dream,
darkling hemisphere, pale and wan
in silver crescent's glow,
swells and ebbs in tidal tempo,
transfixed by the rising lunar splendor.

Cynthian halo sheds frosty beams
glistening downward, striking blue pools,
piercing undead shadows
of ancient conquest.
Moon seas beckon, their waveless shores
mute and arid
await the coming of rain.

Ungirdled loins sway
in restive need of sterile quarry,
lithe star spangled limbs
span the velvet heavens,
silver huntress Diana
unbends slender crescent arms,
looses the gleaming arrow,
unknowing, unerring, the missile
fies to the mark,
unflinching, her prey falters
in fatal ecstasy,
a pleasure alloyed
with endless pain.

A Poet's Fate

Although my soul may depart in darkness,
it shall live always in my poesy's light,
for I have loved shaping verse too warmly
ever to fear the cold eternal night.

Christine

Soft body in dusk's hard light,
pale and selfishly bled,
form and substance reduced
under woe's shroud ill spread.

Remains in day's ebbing light,
her warmth so coldly spread.
Candles lit in disarray,
love's scent long since fled.

When one knows such beauty,
a fire that does not ensue,
his need is thus incomplete
and mourns the love undue.

Ashes in the moon's cool light,
love's traces longtime fled,
fresh from heart's cold oven -
no room in her empty bed.

John Newlin

Artists

She paints with oils
and water too
on taut canvas
with flat and stroke brushes
guided by her mind's eye.

He paints with his thoughts
and dreams too
with nimble keystrokes
on a flat screen
guided by his heart's eye.

She and he are artists,
they both see things,
not as they are,
but as they should be
or could be, by and by.

The Metaphor

During a walk up the beach one day
I saw a young couple lying there
stretched out on a blanket on the sand
with not a worry nor troubling care.

Close by ocean's edge they could hear
the creep of conquest by flooding tide
emulating their loving bond
as they touched and laughed side-by-side.

He, her minstrel, guitar in hand,
she, his lady smiling so fair,
they, two joined souls above it all,
the conficts, the pain and the blare.

As I passed, she smiled up at me
to let me know she understood
my camera had just captured
a metaphor for "life is good."

Paradox

Lightless days and dark free nights,
a monochromatic rainbow display
of heatless fire and tearless keen
and empty heart rive with dismay.

Soundless voices in crescendo,
tasteless sipping of sweet red wine,
numb fingertips knowing soft skin,
sightless eyes viewing the divine.

These things as stated may be true
or not - yet the context still shocks
all but the poet whose sly device
is to employ the paradox.

Sometime

Somewhere or other there must surely be
a face not yet seen, a voice not yet heard.
a heart not yet knowing anything of me,
nor knowing my verse - rhyme nor word.

Someplace or other, maybe near or far,
there shall be, before tomorrow's flight,
beyond the pain of her wandering star,
reminding me of her every night.

Sometime or other, maybe far or near,
the wall, built so long ago, shall come down
and before I go, once again to hear gasps
while exploring beneath a lover's gown.

We Danced

She wanted me up
I wanted her down
and so we danced
round and round.

She wanted me right
I wanted her left
and so we danced,
differences bereft.

We formed a circle
and met round about
and so we danced
with and without

all the pain
and all the glory
that comes with dancing
to such a simple story.

Distant Affections

We met
so many years ago.
I wrote a thousand words,
in a hundred poems
and letters
now tucked away
in her cardboard box.

I should have learned
how to coil up in a ball
and sleep alone at night
under the distant stars.

I might have learned
from the frustrations
of remote affections falling
into her black hole of selfishness.

But the consequences
of that failed experiment
in bridging the distance
will remain with me
all the days of my life.

John Newlin

We Leap

Mendacity deceives honesty
so we leap
from conclusion
to conclusion.

Confusion deceives common sense
so we leap
from platitude
to platitude.

Faith deceives nothing
so we leap
from miracle
to miracle.

Intolerance deceives love
so we leap
from stereotype
to stereotype.

Arrogance deceives propriety
so we leap
from envy
to envy.

Does anyone know
the way to leap
from truth
to truth?

The Challenge

The challenge that awaits you
is nothing less and nothing more
than all of your hopes and your dreams
on the other side of doubt's door.

So take a moment to reflect
on the value of respite and rest
and when you rise on the morrow
strive to give nothing but your best.

Two Ships

Two ships pass closely in the night
when one is hailed with interest's light.
the other, veiled and less than contrite,
sails on, missing the best of life.

Too Much

He made love to her.

Afterwards, they lay
a long time side by side;
he stretched out as if dead
while her body vibrated
like a plucked harp string.

Finally, he looked
into the dark wells
of her liquid eyes
and asked the question:

"Why can you not commit?"

And then, to her silence spoke:
"Please, tell."

She answered, "You love me too much."

He drew her close and said:
"Never too much. Too much is not enough."

But he knew it was too much
and that she soon would go.
And go she did,
taking her love with her,
leaving him alone
to cope with his.

Vertigo

When down is up
and up is down
and all is spinning
round and round,

try to gain some footing
on the trembling ground
when down masquerades as up
and up is disguised as down,

and the dizzying whirling,
the drumbeat sound
that sends you reeling
when you're upside down.

Falling then is soaring
into the profound
downside of up,
where blurred thoughts abound.

Drop anchor, if you can,
when your balance is unwound,
hold fast to the thought,
or life's maze will confound

all your hopes, your dreams
of fame and renown,
of swimming through life,
striving not to drown.

Collapse the Night

Sometimes it is so hard
to get through the long night,
the unforgiving night,
with daunting memories
that haunt my dreamless plight.

The mantle of darkness
congeals the ripe shadows
of long lost devotions,
concealing any escape
from mangled emotions.

Dawn is a desperate wish
of a sleepless wanderer
in the valley of regret
where the arid streams
parch all desires unmet.

A tumultuous silence
resounds in my bedroom.
With no rest, no respite
I mouth a godless prayer,
oh please, collapse the night.

John Newlin

Faith and Fear

Faith is belief in something
that cannot be proven.
So, at times, some trust in the words
of those they have never known.

They believe in the promises
of the those who might enlighten them.
They rely on the feelings
of their family and their friends.

They blindly trust in those
whose promises are filtered
through sermons and verses
from talking pulpits.

But when times get hard
and there is uncertainty and doubt,
faith begins to morph into fear
and fear rushes in to take its place.

Fear is the consummate lever
of mindless political power,
as the wizard behind the curtain
masquerades in faith's place.

After eight years of fear
the electorate is paralyzed
like a deer caught in the headlights
at the end of the future's tunnel.

Road kill then becomes the metaphor
for a great nation brought to its knees
by its dependence on faith
and its addiction to fear.

The Precipice

He followed her
up from the valley below
and walked with her
along burbling brooks,
up through leafy bowers,
and above shifting sands,
climbing the path of love.

The felicity of their walk
was as sinuous as the way
through the forests and glades,
as tenuous as the quicksilver breeze,
as unrequited as the happiness
he refused to accept
at the precipice.

Winter Pain

She touched his hand
as they listened
to the sounds of the snow
softening the ground.

She wanted to tell him
how she had come to be,
who she was...

About her life, about the world,
the way of her in the cold,
under the icey dogwood petals,
the way her love had taken wing.

He listened
but she sensed
he did not hear.

His silence was polar,
his smile frigid,

like leaves vibrating
in the cold wind,
a panic shivered within her.

At that awful moment
She knew that he would go.

And go he did.

The Poet's Table

The poet's table is set
with simile and metaphor,
and alliteration at hand,
much rendition to adore.

And there to freely sup and dine
on the bard's versified geste;
to taste the lyric minstrel's fare
is to to know the fate of the blessed.

Cyber Poetry

We write of things that matter
and some that do not
with words easily said -
can analysis be worthwhile?

Is this a one-act play
in the theater
of the flat screen mind?

And this room is softly faded
and I only sense your shadow -
I cannot feel your hand.

We are fleshless strangers
indulging ourselves
in circumcised peroration.

Memories

When the road that lies ahead
is shorter than the one behind,
we learn to embrace and treasure
each sip of our past, best refined.

So each day fill your empty cup
with memory's sweet reward,
and taste all its latent flavors,
before the last to be poured.

Forgiveness

Forgiveness is borne
in tender loving hands
held out to bended knee
with open palms,

with no harsh word
to disturb the peace
of the ghosts
it puts to rest.

Sometimes it glows,
an aura of white,
lighting the corners
of a darkened hope.

Sometimes it warms,
like a knitted shawl
tenderly draped
over repentant shoulders.

Sometimes it is absent,
an absolution denied
by one who believes
it is only for everyone else.

John Newlin

Last Notes

The brilliance of his poetry
was eclipsed only
by the banality
of her love.

She was a bird
Whose abhorrence
of a nest
doomed every suitor.

The discordance
of her music's last notes
left him scarred and battered
and set her free.

Treasures

Treasures, carefully collected
from the depths of a smitten mind,
finally put in their rightful place,
so quickly forgotten, left behind.

Undated photographs torn in half
burning on the pyre of one's fear,
the flames flickering with regret,
evaporating each feckless tear.

Words altered slyly in mid-flight,
cloaked in the sound of unpledged sighs,
delivered across the senseless void,
on the wings of expectation's demise.

Secrets of frustrated desire lost,
masquerading as passion's needs,
dissolve into wistful mists borne
on the stream of love's fickle breeze.

The Drowning

A spinster found a swimming man,
and chose him to be her very own.
Then she pressed herself close to him,
and dragged him under and far down
into the depths of her selfishness,
where real lovers always drown.

Ivory and Ebony (for George Shearing)

When he seated himself on the bench
the crowd would hush
as he extended long arms,
each ending with five sighted fingers.

Ivory keys alternating with ebony,
groups of octaves, daring those fingers
to use or abuse them at his will,
never a square peg in music's round hole.

The touch of his fingertips on the keys
jolted him, spurred him to reach down
into the deep well of his feelings,
allowing his spirit to make the music.

Like a deep flowing river
the notes streamed from his soul,
commanding his fingers
to sound each splendid chord.

His fingers owned that keyboard,
the ivory and ebony he had never seen,
his mind owned the music,
his milky eyes owned nothing.

He was blind.

The Insult

Silence is a message, a la carte,
unheard words dissing another's art,
so telling of the need to be apart
from the truth lurking in one's heart.

The insult is taken in knowing stride,
the slings and arrows of the past abide
in the dark memories of hope denied
and where ambivalence doth now reside.

The Mystery

I would write a poem
and send it on to thee
could I find nouns and verbs
that explain the mystery

of red feathered arrows,
flying to intended mark;
of narcotic music
mesmerizing the dark;

of importuning doves
each bearing a thornless rose,
of giddy walks a'reeling,
from sultry desire exposed;

of diaphanous dreams,
hypnotic visions nigh,
nightly perspiration,
yearning's effort doth supply;

but the muse avoids me,
words flee this smitten mind,
therefore all that is sent
Is my love -- unrefined.

Regrets

Living is friendlier than dying
but there is always a price.

If you live long enough
there will be times to remember
and times to forget
and you will know
the ghosts of regret.

And the ones
that haunt you the most
are those where you knew
you had a choice,

those where you knew
you might have reined yourself in,
those where you looked into your mirror
and everything solid and sane
about yourself looked back
and said, "Stop."

But you looked away,
and held your course.

Those are the regrets
that will haunt you
all the days of your life.

On The Beach

On a Mendocino beach
two lovers walked hand in hand,
and laughed and teased as they strolled
along the kelp strewn sand.

She picked up a crooked stick
and in the sand she traced
their fondest sobriquets,
one day to be disgraced.

She the queen of spinsters,
his perverted paramour.
He the pedantic prick,
her spelling to deplore.

That day lives in but one heart,
a heart that wears pain's frown,
a heart promising one day,
to gift her with a special crown.

A Glass of Wine

Ahhh, a glass of wine,
liquid fruit so devine,
a dry vintage sublime.

A love song entertaining
whispered words painting
a gentle suitor's campaigning.

And when the bottle is drained,
each delicious taste retained,
ardor's pleasure is unrestrained.

The Poet's Conundrum

There go I
where I would
and if not
I shall not
wish that I would not
ever be what I am not
and desire love
from whom I may
that I must not.

So here go I
where I know not
to be one
with the sun
among those
who care not
and those
who see not.

So there went I
where I grew not
wanted not
of the wisdom
of those who cared
and those who
meant a lot.

Paper Airplane

A paper airplane in mid-air,
dreams below buried in the sand,
aerodynamics impaired,
the loss of altitude unplanned.

When one is driven from the sky,
while drifting to the beach below,
he abandons the game, the lie,
and places all his bets on show.

The beach is made from time's sand,
the sea foams over each grain
like cotton candy on the strand
of tidal dreams dissolved in vain.

Frail paper wings on dead air
floating across an empty beach,
destination tomorrow's dare,
beyond yesterday's empty reach.

Christmas Day

Unlock the door to your heart,
share the gentleness within.
Open the window of your soul
and let the new year's hope rush in.

No matter that you've traveled,
nor if you're so very far away,
the memory of you, close and dear,
shall bring cheer on Christmas day.

John Newlin

They

They stood at their headland,
arm in arm, sometimes gazing back
to the way they had come,
over the plateau, through the thorns,
past the wreckage
wrought by their words
and erosive deeds.

Side by side they stood in silence.

Beyond them lay their future,
rolling and breaking
like barbarous waves
over the the rocks and shoals
of their divergent expectations.

Within them, their dreams,
spiked with spiteful thoughts,
like shards of broken glass,
guarding the wall tops
set around them,
denying not only entrance
but escape.

Their uneven strengths
clashed on the battleground
of love offended,

where each was betrayed
by a selfish will
that no pair could survive,
least of all they.

John Newlin

Love's Wheel

I have thus decided that
it is not possible to love
someone who is less than real.

Love is far too ephemeral
and so incandescently rash
that it cannot help but seal

all the hope and all the trust
burned and charred into ashes
to be buried with ardor's zeal.

Perhaps I should withhold my troth
to avoid being swiftly ground
as hapless grist for love's cruel wheel.

Rise and Fall

Beyond the arid ravine
the plain rolled up
to the base of the mountain.

Through the dense cloud
rose it's the purple cone,
flanked by the snowy summits
of its ancient siblings.

They stood there together
for an icy eternity,
not quite holding hands.
as remotely distant
as the frigid peaks
beyond them.

The heights of their knowing
had been scaled
and the wounds of the ascent
would never heal.

Then their descent
into the valley
down opposite slopes
through the murky clouds
of despair
left each alone
in an angry sea
of denial.

John Newlin

An Unwritten Poem

An unwritten poem, a verse,
poignant complaint in reckless style,
a deft presence once here, now fled,
deceptive as a lover's smile.

Was it caprice or just false glow
that brought me joy, or was it grief?
Among the debris of time I searched,
seeking the illusion, love's thief.

Her eyes mirrored the future
a glacial vista never planned,
so inscrutably transient
like silly scribbling in the sand.

Each day grows shorter, pencil thin,
as I stroll through the pelting rain,
ever spattered but not yet wrung
from my immersion in the pain.

Once I was filled with her magic
but dark remembrance clouds the air,
knowing that my future depends
on forgetting she was ever here.

Yet I shall taste that cake again
with sweeter icing flowing down,
bright ink on the nib of the pen,
new verses from old muse's crown.

In the cold rejection
of unrequited thought,
twittering like a bird's harsh
taunting song overwrought,

a lover might conclude
that a single wing and prayer
are sincere partners
in surviving dead air,

but trust and investment
in a spinster's shrewd art
shall surely result
in a hole in one's heart.

Gethsemane

The agony of betrayal had begun.

"Am I the seed of my father?" asked the son,
"Or am I but a random drop of sorrow flung
down in the dust from which mankind hath sprung?"

The answer elevated him on his last day
to the wooden tower of his triumphant dismay.

The Stone Garden

Row on alabaster row,
gleaming in the summer sun,
pale in the moon's lambent light,
each name starkly carved, unsung.

Thousands of silent markers
metaphors for what lay below,
each life so ill-remembered,
in formation - row on row.

The soil accepts, embraces
each warrior's broken life,
like the arms of a mother
or thoughts of a grieving wife.

And year after fateful year
the stones shall endure the moss,
and long after the last service,
who shall kneel to mourn the loss?

Row on alabaster row,
under the care of God's warden,
the saddest place on this earth
is the beautiful stone garden.

Our Days

To the wonderful days that were
and to empty days that were not;
I recall the ambivalence
of loving hours, so dearly bought.

Times of care and times of knowing,
all our history was so discrete,
never daring to embrace
the possibility of defeat.

How to keep the music playing,
how to roll love's honest dice,
how to sustain a fragile faith,
finding some way to sacrifice?

Love's wine became a concoction
that could never be safely brewed
in the deep vat of commitment
without being thus misconstrued.

So I lift my empty glass
in tribute to us and speak:
I wish you were here to dry
the tears on my weathered cheek.

Verse

In order to converse
with the universe
one might
consider the inverse
of the obverse
or vice-versa.

But to remain diverse
it is best to reverse
the adverse nature
of the perverse.

Which, of course,
describes the true nature
of satirical verse.

Colors

Is there is a palette
on which the balance
of the additive colors
in our world
are in harmony with
their subtractive counterparts?

Where the sharp
divisions of conflict
are blurred with pastels
that melt away
the fear and trauma
with smooth indelible strokes
of human color
that can never fade?

Alas, if not
then our world
shall always be
a bleak sphere conflicted
by shades of black and white.

Climb a Tree

Climb a tall tree, look to the west,
throw back your head, defy the wind,
laugh when you think of all the rest
who do not care when time began.

Wade gayly in the bubbling stream,
prance along the sun-drenched lane,
twirl in you silks like a dancing queen
while praying you'll fly home again.

Broken wings ache forever,
broken promises hurt just a day,
yet they stay the true endeavor
of she who has lost her way.

Cold Memory

She stepped out
into the raw night.

Clear ice rattled crisply
on the dry leaves
still clinging
to the black oaks.

Broken clouds scudded
across the misty crescent
of the moon.

The cold embraced her
like an old friend,
blanched but true.

She shivered
and wrapped herself
in the cold memory
of his warm hands
removing the plait
from her silken hair.

Then she turned
and stepped back
into the quiet room
where his framed medals
commanded the mantel
over the fireplace.

She walked slowly
through the flickering shadows
cast by the dying flames
to where he lay
so still and silent
in the final warmth
and safety
of his casket.

John Newlin

The Glass

The crystal glass,
a brilliant array
of diamond cuts,
once unbreakable,
once full.

The glass, once full
of wine pressed
from the sweetest
ripe grapes of
our driest memories.

We filled the vessel,
the goblet of life
and sanguine love,
grasping the stem,
tipping the base.

Then it was half emptry,
it's ruby brilliance
thus decayed,
yet we drank together
and toasted our lives.

The glass now is empty
and there is no more
to decant and pour
from the bottle of who
once we were.

The Colorist

She searched the shelves of her heart
and discovered hiding there
her poetic crayons -
all her colors, true and fair.

She opened up the cupboard
where the drawing paper lay
and on a sheet began to sketch
the shades of her heart's bouquet.

The pastels freely flowed,
into a rainbow's reflection
of her only remembrance
of love's spectral perfection.

The rainbow arc of her crayons,
was hers only to convey,
and those who dare deny it,
their own defects display.

John Newlin

Life

Life is only
a long disease
with but one termination.

It's last years
are appalling;

racked by pains,
senses going;
loves, friends, occupation
dissolving...

an old man must pray
for imbecility
or a heart of stone
to defend

the unspeakable
levity with which
the faint chance of happiness
is thrown away for some tiff,
some remote sullenness
of private vanity.

His mistaken sense of honour,
the weak and deadly notion
that inhabits his decrepit heart
is all the armor he has to don
in the final hour of battle.

The Scent of Darkness

Not having slept in darkness,
he watched the birth of day.

Its first light gathered stealthily,
like a thief in a gray cloak.

As the light grew bolder,
the mountains emerged,
their craggy shoulders
still clinging to the dark of night.

The warmth of the pregnant morning
melted away the wisps of fog
clinging to the peaks like cobwebs
spun across purple gables.

Down in the lea the shapes of trees
were still glistening
in drops of stubborn dew.

He rose and walked down his path,
the scent of darkness still lingering
in the morning of his mind.

John Newlin

Ambivalence

Ambivalence - the best and worst
of never saying very much
about one's private universe.

Attitudes versus feelings play
on every thought, every touch
that keep confessions at bay.

Truths rarely grace trained lips,
instead escape one's clutch
in the form of casual quips.

Make no choice come what may,
straddle the fence and never rush
lest a bad choice your heart betray.

That Night

We felt one another's mind;
love came to us as birth does,
knowing its own time better
than the waiting for it.

In that night,
my own life left me
to live in her.

With all before,
I had been myself alone.
yet I learned from her trust
and that was enough.

By daybreak
we had forgotten,
the need of words
and she smiled at me
and held my hand.

John Newlin

Then She Was Gone

I knew her by everything,
by the set of her shoulders,
the lilt of her smile,
the light wispy hair
of her temples.

I knew her face
in the light of the low sun
and like the shadow of a dream,
all my life sped by.

Her head tilted back
in laughter;
it was a thing
to stop a heart.

I tasted her image,
I drank her reality,
it was of wine and honey.

One New Year's day
she promised to love me more,
an empty promise.

The next year she was gone.
I can still hear the clicking
of the high-booted heels
of her flying footfalls.

For Alisha

If I were really, really tiny
I'd lasso a bumblebee

and nestle in it's soft fur
and buzz over the flowery sea.

If I could talk to a Jay bird
with feathers gray and blue

I would ask him kindly to tell
his relatives to visit you.

If I were huge and gigantic
I'd hold my long arms up high

and catch a wandering planet
as it went orbiting by.

But I guess that when God made me
he knew the nature of my art,

and so I've been made just right
to hold a niece within my heart.

Time Warp

Tomorrow was so long ago
that I know not how many years
were destined on that first day.

Yesterday began tomorrow
but tomorrow is yet to come,
so how can I know the way

through the timeless scenes
of growing old and thinking young
in the last acts of this play?

The future's past is the past's future
or so it seems when contemplating
the remaining time's decay.

Never mind, I shall surely be
out of time on that fated day
when rainbows dim and fade to gray.

Tennessee Valley

We walked hand-in-hand through the oaks,
on a winding trail through time's debris,
down through the Tennessee Valley
to where the black sand greets the sea.

Standing there, on the edge of time,
I thought we would never end,
locked together, forever tied
by fate's unfathomable whim.

There are places from which we came,
and those that we might yet discern
that would define that certain place
to which we may never return.

At night, when loneliness whispers
to me of that indelible stroll,
I'm a prisoner of remembrance
and I pray for my swift parole.

John Newlin

Revenge

Revenge is the slave of a narrow mind
that serves its master with poisonous art,
that concocts the deadly effect combined
with the acid tears from a broken heart.

Vengeance is the cloak of an empty soul
that protects the vanity of ire's whim
and encourages spite's malicious goal
of fomenting the maelstrom deep within

that once gentle heart of a lover gone
from the day, from the sun, from everywhere,
whose own retribution was love withdrawn
in a final manner, cruel and unfair.

So, from day to mortal day I survive,
contriving vengeance in every way
to inflict the pain of memory's drive
with no hope of restoring yesterday.

Some Things

At the end of the day
there are some things
that cannot be helped.

Some things
we don't want to hear
and some things we say
because we can't hold
our silence any longer.

Some things said
are more than need be said -
maybe sometimes less;
there are things one does
and things one may say
because one makes a choice.

Some things perhaps
need be kept to oneself,
yet every now and then
some things are spoken
in the wake of selfish thought.

Some things, once said,
cannot be taken back
yet can be forgiven
if hearkened by the ear
of one who knows
a thing or two.

John Newlin

Over There

Consider the cost should you dare,
three thousand American trees felled
in that bloody desert over there.

Our blood soaks the sands, over there,
in spite of the sound of protest
permeating the people's prayers.

Mothers dread the night and their dreams
of the blood and gore in the sand,
knowing that only they hear their screams.

Sons and brothers, starkly aware
of their mother's enduring grief,
question the why of over there.

His answer comes down cold and clear,
they must nobly die over there
to not meet that fate over here.

But if people speak without fear
ignoble thoughts of over there,
it cannot happen over here.

Babylon's Fields

In Babylon's fields the sands blow
between the crosses row on row,
that mark our place; and in the sky
vultures, soaring and singing, fly
serenading the guns below.

We are the Dead. Short days ago
we lived, felt dawn, saw sunset glow,
loved and were loved, and now we lie
in Babylon's fields.

We had no quarrel with the foe:
yet our failed leader's hands did throw
the challenge; ours to do or die.
For noble cause, our leader's lie,
we shall not sleep, though sands do blow
in Babylon's fields.

What If?

What if we had been aligned
as true soul mates?

and then

when our day finally came,
I saw you for all the splendor you were
and ignored the spinster in you.

And so

we might have been a we,
each committed to our youth betrayed
in lusty misalignment and fool's play,
had we but known what little we knew,
perhaps we might still be a we.

But since

each day's bitter memories
coat me in varnished regret
so little time left to dream
of rocking chair memories.

And now

I would trade all the world I have seen
and all the places I have been,
to taste again those moments before
I knew you did not love me.

And you, what of you?

You who sailed
so blithely at the helm
of the flagship of my love,
basking in your need
of a spinster's freedom.

   And so it goes.

Do you sometimes wish,
as ever I do,

that we had never met?

John Newlin

The Glass

When is the glass half full?
When is it half empty?

Perhaps it's about
knowing why to say when
and when to say why.

The demarcation
is a line that floats
like a barometer
of needs and desires,
moving up and down
as the pressure changes.

Perhaps it's about who's pouring
and depends upon
what's being poured.

Is all we want just a taste?

Or is the glass bottomless
and too much is never enough?

Life's Debris

When stopping to smell the roses
be not least mindful of the thorn,
lest the prick of old devotions
revive keening memories ill-worn.

For each memory has its twin,
darkness to light, pain to pleasure;
summoning one, not the other,
denying each the fullest measure

of the remembrance of each day
whether choosing to bruise and break
or to bless the blossoms and divine
the sentient debris in life's wake.

The Bereaved

His father stood alone
on a hill that overlooked
a dale that harbored a lea
of grassy turf, hallowed sod.

Below, his numbed gaze found
row on row of alabaster crosses
gleaming in the eternal
sheen of the midday sun.

One marked his seed,
...and his lost hope.

The day waited solemnly
while he contemplated
the laying to rest of
his son's patriotic contempt
for his own mortality.

Lady of the Night

Blessed be the ardor
of violet words
uttered in the heat of night,
whispered untrimmed,
urgent as convulsion's
approaching strains.

Where is the one
who tripped in heels,
turned on the lathe
of the procurer's sloth,
ebbing with age?

Truth dissolves the mists,
banishes yesterday's lies,
lifts the curtain of darkness
to starkly reveal
the procurer's delight
is no longer there.

The lady of the night
at last is free.

John Newlin

Satchmo

It was big, but never easy
for the gifted orphan
who was born in the glow
of the red lights dotting
the Back o' Town area
of the Big Easy

He learned to sing
and tested his lips
on the cornet
in reform school.

He and his Easy style
of music stormed
and captured the nation
and the world
but his heart never left
his Crescent City.

He rests now
below dry, green grass
in Flushing Cemetary
far from the devastated city
where Satchmo and jazz
were born.

He would raise his
gravely voice to sing
"What a Wonderful World"
in honor of those who strive
to save his beloved city.

But his trumpet would
never sound Taps.

Fallen Statues

In those endless, passionate nights,
lying side-by-side in the darkness,
toppled statues of ourselves,
we sought escape
from the intolerable present
through the past,
the warm blanket of the past.

We reprised our earlier days,
reminding, correcting, censuring
like ancient adversaries
stumbling hand-in-hand
toward the door of a place
we had once lived,
long, long ago.

Then the door opened
and we came undone,
clay feet crumbling like
the promises issued
from invisible tongues
in sightless heads.

Life and Limb

His buddy had a life, but
in one explosive moment
it went in all directions,
leaving his shattered body
behind.

Tattered uniform,
life's spattered blood,
soaking the sandy ground,
the shock made him drunker
than the night before.

He knelt beside his friend
and reached out,
his love guiding the arm
that was no longer there.

The bloody curtain
of the last act
had not descended
until someone gently
stayed his shredded arm
and led him away.

Serena From Verbena

The leader of the band
was nutty as the Stuckeys
along the road to Verbena
where he booked a gig
at the Hillbilly Cafe.

Along the way
we picked up a voice
in Clanton.

Serena from Verbena,
a black chick with white eyes
and a purple voice
like maple syrup poured
through river bottom gravel.

We opened with "Evil Gal Blues"
and my alto Selmer 80
must have thought
it heard an Allora bari
'cause it nearly jumped
off the strap when
Serena's voice strangled that room
with the whispy threads
of her foggy voice.

Couldn't help but watch her
as she pressed the mike to her lips
and sang, never moving anything
but her shoulders in rhythm
to the beat of that tune.

Funny how a band can instantly
flow with a new voice.
We eagerly plunged into the
muddy river of her talent
and sensed the hypnotic effect
she had on our audience.

I heard she was on parole,
meth and other stuff,
and as the night got darker
her need thickened her voice
and left it's sheen on her brow.

She left before the last set,
gone without a word,
just grabbed her pay,
off to score a victory
which sadly was her defeat.

John Newlin

The Sax Man

Along the way to our
gig at Cooper's Hillbilly Cafe
we picked up a baritone voice
in Clanton.

Damn!
He was as big as a mountain
a black man with white eyes
whose Allora bari
blew with a purple voice
like maple syrup poured
through a river bottom's gravel.

We opened with "Evil Gal Blues"
and my alto Selmer 80
nearly jumped
off the strap when
his horn's voice strangled that room
with the whispy threads
of it's foggy voice.

I loved that voice
and I hated it too,
'cause his instrument
was bigger than mine
but so was his heart.

I swore that next season
I'd buy me a baritone.
Too bad I coudn't buy
me a big beautiful black body
with a roiling muddy heart
as well.

John Newlin

A Sweet Gig

A sweet gig in Montgomery,
we followed the Moonshine Cherries
and left while Ziggy was packing in.

We took up a fiddler in Birmingham,
got to have a fiddler in bubba-land
our leader said.

Didn't much care
for the idea myself,
but the club said it would pay.

Just before the opening set,
fiddler's palm caressed his strings;
their whispers told me all was well.

He backed us with
soft and sweet refrains,
and we settled in.

He began his solo
bowing, some strange notes,
seemingly random,
heading somewhere unknown.

Over and over like
they made little sense,
unrelated, dissonant.

A sound as scrumpy
as the hard cider
pressed in the back woods.

Suddenly he gathered them up
into a startling variation
and fingers and bow began to fly.

He had found the line he was seeking
and he followed the notes where they led,
as sweet and easy as blackberry pie.

That rhythmic run of resonant notes
had our audience swaying, foot-tapping,
and nodding to his seductive bowing.

With the butt of his fiddle braced
on his broad chest he beat out the rhythm
on the strings with his bow.

The place was rockin' and bumpin'
and nobody in the place that night
was into his music more than the band.

During the next set, his playing
was softer and more pensive,
which subdued the mood
but elevated the spirit.

His minor key would float in
like a rustling of the wind,
through the trees at twilight.

When the gig was done, he went his way,
the way of audiences, clubs, and the rain,
but the sound of that fiddle lingers.

Maybe next time we play bubba-land
we'll call Charley from Clanton
to sit in and remind us
what red-neck jazz is all about.

I lost Her

I lost her in the shadows
so I tuned my heart to the shade,
to the music we shared at night,
the empty promises she made.

Dancing away through the blue night
she escaped my gaze, laughing, gay,
and the sound of her last words
still burn in the coldest way.

John Newlin

Evening in Babylon

The Marine was reflective
as he bent to his letter,
dotting his I's
like his mates at muster,
crossing his t's,
like alabaster crosses--
it seemed his entire world
was being crucified.

He paused, feeling a qualm.
His letter was slanting downhill
and he hoped to live
until he could post it.

He looked up, it was dark once again,
the eve of another scorching day
when more American blood
would anoint the sands of Babylon.

Frustrated by lapses of sanity,
he shuddered with primordial fear,
dreading the sound of the failures
of body armor on the morrow.

He could not escape the sounds,
sounds unlike the healthy tumult
of home in America, where he belonged,
but like the cries of freedom's marchers
wreathing in agony.

He knew that morning
would too soon be announced
by the howls of the pariah dogs
and the cacophony of the cocks.
The screaming and moaning
would come later
in the bloody heat of Babylon's day.

He capped his pen,
plugged his ears,
snuffed out the light,
and prayed to be spared
inevitable daybreak --
but he did not sleep.

Freedom's quixotic disaster
never sleeps in Babylon.

John Newlin

Babylon's Honor

I think of our dead -
and theirs -
heaped in the dust
by their ancient river.

I hear the howls
of the wolves and jackals
who sent them.

I knew that other hands before theirs
had sealed our warrior's deaths;
the sword hand of the Chief
guided by those on his right,
sworn to bloody fealty.

He set out on his war,
and we heard only of one foe,
his father's enemy -
he looked to avenge his honor.

Did he rejoice in the stumps
of those returning without limbs?

He avoided the solemnity
of the star-spangled caskets -
no honor there.

One by one each limb fell
in spite of the trust.

We can feel their scars
and our honor is dismembered
along with our warrior's bodies.

And the flesh and blood
of our sons and daughters
drench the sands of Babylon.

For whose honor?

The Good Life

Cigarette tips glowed
like fireflies
in the smokey darkness
of the club.

The drummer was high,
Sugar Kane, the bassist,
was drunk.
Never saw the pianist before,
but he had major fingers.

Neon lightning flashed
through the dirty window
as our sounds tested
the thinness of the peeling paint
on the smoke-stained walls.

The crowd swayed quietly
in their rickety chairs,
the ultimate praise
of our gift to their ears.

At the end of each set,
there would be
a spattering of applause -
they had already
paid their dues.

At the end of the evening,
when our patrons were long gone,
we sat together,
eyeing each other over a beer,
and talked quietly
of how good life is.

Mystery of the Horn

The mystery of the horn
is learned and not born.

Dynamic articulation rules,
in all the universal schools.

How to exploit your love on stage,
two and one-half octaves range.

Fingering is much you need to know
of venting through your horn's soul.

Vibrato, subtones, ghosting, falls,
turns, and bending all the rules.

Melodic minors, ascending scale,
blow and blow until you are pale.

Middle E is sweet and clear,
at least to my gin-soaked ear.

Consensual Sax

In the smoky midnight hour
at the N'orleans Blue Nile
on Frenchman Street,
we danced, hip to hip,
swaying bodies, grazing lips.

From the stage
the sax player's breath
rendered his magic riffs
with a heartfelt touch,
floating, teasing above
the rich, husky line
of the thrumming bass.

Soaking in the sweet jazz,
through the late musky hour
we lost ourselves in misty time
while drifting on the liquid sound
of that consensual sax.

The Going

He gazed ruefully down at her.
She had feathery raven hair,
translucent skin and green eyes
above a ripe, ample bosom.

She narrowed her moistening eyes
as she turned to look up at him.

Her delicate lashes swept up;
her face, like an innocent child's,
showed realization - and fright.

The scent of her fear puzzled him,
though a mirror might have told him.

A lone tender string in his heart
vibrated for her, a still dirge -
then he turned, ready to go...

but he paused for a brief moment
as the doorway became a frame
for the portrait of her beauty.

She looked so intensely fragile,
too smooth to touch, like an egg of a dove;
her pale, parted lips pursed and silent.

She had been such a sweet taste
after so many bitter sips,
yet he knew he would never
decant her liquid love again.

And then he was gone.

John Newlin

The Asylum

Was it the absence
of the music that made it
so strange that his body
was swaying to its rhythm?

Was he yearning for the lilt
of a timeless dance
that had long since
surrendered its tempo?

Lurking in the asylum grounds,
madness sometimes ceased to be
a refuge from reality,
leaving him to become incarnate
with its insentient lucidity.

Can a madman find sanity
in such a place?
Where reason, inexorably numb,
might invert his mind?

Could no one share
his burden of conscience
or plumb the duality
of his indelible sorrow?

No one ever dared,
not even his keepers.

Best Friend

A bottle of gin, a moist reed,
a circle of fifths along the way
to keep in loving touch
with all the sharps and flats
married to the keys.

A horn on the strap
is more pliable
than a woman in bed
and the altissimo register
is a far better friend.

The Rose

The scent of a lovely rose,
hard plucked and rudely scorned
lingers in the heart's garden,
as sharp as ever his thorn.

The little crown so ravaged,
its fragile petals descend,
wafting down the thin dead air,
his betrayal to attend.

She may rise and bloom again
should she cut and bravely prune
the dead cane from the living
and cauterize the dreadful wound.

Wallflower

Too tall, too thin, too flat,
too shy to twirl or flirt,
a pale sensitivity
in her ankle-length skirt.

Desire, on hold, beneath
a chiffon petticoat
unseen, unknown, by his
censored heart remote.

The Belle

I would don her lyric skirt
but it shrinks at the fit;
I reach for the Belle's pen
but it will not submit.

I seek to know her truth
but it yields not to me,
and with complaint I pray
her muse one day agree

to a footnote obscure
beneath her verse sublime,
even though my thin ink stains
the page with unkempt rhyme.

John Newlin

Vacancy

In the shadow cast by her fleeing,
at the end of love's darkest day,
there is something to spurn,
something to allow
to slip away.

In the dark corner of each evening,
in the vacant silence of the wind
there is much to remember --
too much to remember
in order to begin again.

I need some shelter,
I need a guide
I am lost at sea.
I am all alone
on the ebbing tide.

The Arabesque

The rhythm is indelible sound,
point your toes and spin round and round
in consonance with its timeless beat,
out-leap the shadow of art's deceit.

The stage is yours, command it well,
use your poise and grace to weave a spell
for vacant eyes in the silent crowd,
summon all of which you are endowed.

One of your legs is straight, not bent,
the other raised behind in consent;
your arms aligned, in harmonious pose
from fingertips to slippered toes.

Intricate moves, geometric dance,
the night and music to enhance;
you shine in your artful quest
to perform the arabesque.
How can I not?

Today & Tomorrow

When today entreats tomorrow
and tomorrow rejects yesterday,
which moment of her denial
should the paradox then betray?

Perhaps it should be that moment,
when facing an unwelcome truth,
one must embrace the numbing pain
injected by her serpent's tooth.

Dignity

"You are dying."

He squirmed at the sight of
the contrast of the white coat
and black name tag.

Fear took him by the hand.

"I want to die with dignity," he replied.

The white coat shrugged,
"You may live with dignity,
but you cannot die with it."

The name tag paled,
the coat darkened.

He left, hand-in-hand,
with his last partner.

John Newlin

You Are a Poet

You are a poet
if your heart
has been to Amherst

and you keep the dew
of old devotions
in a Grecian urn.

You are a poet
because you know a maid
that's been ruined

and because the fireflies
glimmering in your yard
are a constellation
of an Irish crowd of stars.

You are a poet
when you can write the saddest lines,
or knowing way leads on to way,
and have doubted the coming back

or you have taken
a ceremonious April walk
with a spinster.

You are a poet
if you have seen
Susanna searching for
the touch of springs,
finding concealed imaginings

and because, when death calls,
you take up the pen and write
"if thou wilt, remember,
and if thou wilt, forget."

I Am a Ship

I am a ship
a wooden hulled vessel
that leaks and creaks and seeks
the embrace of a calm harbor.

I have sailed
too close to the wind,
surrendered too much leeway,
and have reveled in too many ports.

My cargo now is baggage
from previous voyages,
musty crates of old devotions,
stacked in memory's hold.

My masts are raked,
the topgallants never reefed.
I seek a fair wind
and yearn for a following sea.

Yet I have been de-masted
and becalmed
and despised like a miscreant
beached in the fickle foam.

My hull may not long sustain
the vagaries of the sea's energy.
I long for a home port
in which to drop final anchor.

A Mother's Goodbye

She clutched the triangular fold
of white stars on a blue field
as she stood on the hallowed ground.

She sang dolefully, with a reverence
that shaped the tremulous tone
of her weary, aging voice.

Her song was thinned by despair
yet was thickened by the memory
of all the years of his youth.

The words drifted on her voice
like curling leaves on the water
of a swirling, muddy creek.

The damp forest absorbed
the resonance of her lyrics,
as if fearing an echo might offend.

When her song ended
its mournful cry was answered
by the plaintive trill of a meadowlark.

She knelt and touched the stone
marking her warrior's place in eternity,
and whispered goodbye to her son.

Sea of Dreams

Each new dream is a voyage,
on a gray, unfathomable sea,
accompanied by phantoms,
drifting in and out of memory's lee.

A wooden helm by which to steer
ignored by the narcotic breeze
and undercurrents of the mind
leaving no sin to be appeased..

Not even the stars can be seen
to navigate the sea of a dream,
nor can a dreamer clearly recall
all the islands in midnight's stream.

Some cold visions bubble up
from memory's timeless deep
to evoke the dreamer's mourning
and to give him cause to weep.

The Way of Dreams

We cannot know
whence come the ephemeral
night visits, staged in the
hynotic theater
of our latent minds.

Nor can we know
what meaning, if any,
each narcotic illusion,
might have in our
capricious lives.

We can only awaken
and marvel at the magic
of the mysterious sequence
of images that drifted
on the river of our sleep.

And sometimes the weight
of a hard day is borne
on the filmy shoulders
of the oldest dream
lurking in one's heart.

L' Auberge

He was a living seed
in a shell knowing
no other world.

Through the white wall
came temptations's light.

He tested the wall,
fearful and unknowing.

Lightning struck his heart,
the shell cracked open.

And he was alive
with her at L'Auberge.

A Sadder Man

A sadder man than I
might complain
that to uncoil the
rhapsodies of the heart
is to risk the fate
of happiness.

A bolder man than I
might assert
that to unfurl
the banners of the soul
is to open the gates
to submissiveness untold.

A braver man than I
might be tempted
to look into
memory's rusted mirror
only to confront the reflection
of the regret and the fear.

The Moon

The sun was gone,
leaving behind,
in the darkness,
the rippling surface
of his reverie.

The moon's face
drifted above the sea
making a lambent swath
reflecting from the
the waves of his thoughts.

He saw the moon
and its passages
as a prescient disc
foretelling the darkening
of his luminous wake.

The Reverie

He felt her cool fingers
on his fevered brow
while he dreamt of her
waking, smiling
in another room
next to another,
washed clean
of the memory of him.

Then he awoke
and wept.

The Prism

The light from his sun
sped through
the transparency
of his prismatic desire,
refracting into a brilliant palette,
a rainbow of his passion.

An array of emotions,
colors of the heart,
hues of the mind,
blending one to the next,
a spectrum of his
sentient being.

Projected onto the cold
wall of the cubicle
of his surrender that
both harbors and imprisons
the light within.

Memories

A kaleidoscope of images...

Some too ephemeral
to survive in the
coldest chamber of
this rash heart.

Some in a warmer place,
ethereal fragments
of a failed past
woven into a gossamer web
glistening with the dewdrops
of a happier time.

Some a panoply
of dusty paintings,
framed in the moldings
of love and affection....

and of regret.

Winter Heart

She smiled
and cocked her head
as she spoke.

Her words seemed to float
over the ocean that separated them
but upon arrival they rained down
like icicles from the eaves
of her winter heart.

She watched through sightless eyes
as the magnitude of her cruelty
overwhelmed him.

He calmly surrendered
to the rush of her vengeance.
It was where they were,
where she needed them to be.

How had they come to this?

A word, just a single word,
uttered in anger by a lover
frustrated by time and distance
to a love who had never known love.

Wide-eyed and beyond redemption,
he shivered in the winter rain
that fell during his going.

He never set eyes on her again...

but she reigns forever as queen
of the winter corner of his heart.

Girl Underwater

The sea embraces her
in its liquid fold serene
and in the silent, swirling depths
cloaks her in a watery dream

Of memories, of old desires,
of nagging, aching fears,
of mysteries and deceptions,
of visions of future years.

Of days of hope, nights of doubt,
of twilight's gloom replete
with a lingering taste of life,
so sweet....yet so bittersweet.

The dream thickens and blurs,
rewards her with knowledge true
that laurel leaves are hers to grasp
in new triumphs to be accrued.

The Two

They did not move
the earth from its axis,
yet a tilt seemed possible.

They were the best
that two could be
at walking, laughing,
at holding hands,
at caressing, loving.

She smiled and danced,
he painted poems
and loved the girl in her;
they were never old.

He cannot look at stars
and not remember
sweet July, their beginning.

Now the world is oblique.
The stars in the dark sky
spell out her name,
light years away.

John Newlin

Epiphany

How does one undo
what has been done
in the name of passion's
rash, dissonant voice?

Could there somewhere be
a quiet, sterile room
where both could go to listen
to an older symphony?

Is there a sanctuary where
an epiphany is honored
with comprehension and respect,
and, oh God please, forgiveness?

The Dance

A swift step forward
and then a slow one back,
then two to the side,
swaying to the beat,
whistling in the dark.

Round and round we go
ever touching, never close,
concealing, revealing,
congealing the hope
that never had a chance.

Her Shoppe

Her shoppe is closed,
its windows sore empty,
the facade full shuttered,
the welcome mat gone.

So where do I go
to spend my love?

John Newlin

How To Die

With her
or without her,
there is no remedy,
for when I am with her
she kills me
and without her I die.

If she wishes me gone
she should stab me,
but not in the heart,
for there she would strike
her own image.

Now each cold sunrise
brings the dry days
and empty nights,
stalked by the thoughts
of mortality.

When I falter
she'll not be
beside my pillow
and without her eyes
fastened on mine
I'll not know how to die.

Another Day

Dawn's cold fingers
touched his damp brow
and lifted the veil
of his uneasy sleep.

It seemed a century since
she was lying there
awaiting the delicacy
of his shoulder kiss.

He stared into the vacancy,
where the warm sense of her
had melted away.

The blow of reality smote him,
before he could rise
and don his rusty armor.

He could hardly bear the pain.

"Christ," he groaned. "Another day."

Upland Promise

We climbed steep winding paths
that tacked about the crags,
up through the misty swaths
that curled through the piney tops,

past rocky slopes,
where our boldest dreams
perched like the nests
of the storks
that delivered them.

At the very top,
above the cloud-dampened woods,
we stood in the barren, stony upland,
breathing the rare air of hope.

Having come so far,
we asked the gods
for us to be charmed
against failure and demise.

The gods silent answer
left us each to know
that we had discarded
reality on the plain
far below.

Later, after our descent,
since our ascendent dreams
had been flattened by defeat
it must be said that the gods
kept their word.

John Newlin

Autumn Heart

I own an autumn heart,
a pumpkin ripened by time,
subliminally carved,
regret's candle burning within.

I harvest the fruits of love
in lemon crates
on a wagon pulled by
a gored ox.

Wobbling in the ruts,
past yesterday's castles,
past frosted fields
of sterile grain.

Past straw sentries,
grinning effigies,
watching the crows
through sightless eyes.

Rumbling over wood decking
creaking in protest,
a grating warning that it is
the bridge of no return.

Autumn's music reigns,
plaintive refrains
vibrating in veinless leaves
destined soon to fall.

Cowled winter awaits,
its frosty greeting
crisp and certain
in its cold, cruel finality.

Firestorm

The hot air is suddenly filled
with flying, sparking embers,
spewing from a volcano
of burning brush.

Tongues of fickle flame
too capricious to predict,
too horrific to accept,
lick at a lifetime of gleaning,

The essence of living
is consumed
in the voracious wildfire;
human cost - biotic loss.

Charcoal remains
mark the lunar landscape
in silent commemoration
of the remains of the loss.

Tall brick chimneys stand,
charred impotent memorials;
sightless monuments to nature's
wrath, immolation and rebirth.

How Could She Not

How could she not?
I'll tell her how.

By fingers too swift
and a tongue too sharp,
governed by a mind
too old, too tart.

By an eye too near
the prize to perceive
that the barb was naught
and trust should believe.

By a heart still lost
from years of neglect,
self incarceration;
and now a love wrecked.

How could she not?
she well knows
her lover faltered,
and she doused the afterglow.

John Newlin

The Recipe

A dash of expectations,
a pinch of dreams,
a teaspoon of hope...

Spicy ingredients,
whisked in the virgin oil
of time...

A piquant dressing
for life's
greening salad...

but perhaps
too pungent for
its dessert.

Dust

Dust in my eyes,
obscuring a hopeful vision,
a dream not dreamt
until dreaming it
became a wind storm
blowing out to the sea
of mortality.

Dust in my heart
scattered there,
casual debris
strewn by a fugitive soul
fleeing from
the consequences
of love.

John Newlin

Demon Dream

I dreamed a demon dream last night,
deep in the abyss, far from light.
A cold dew soaked my fearful brow
when her form appeared somehow
in the dank folds of my empty bed,
"Do you dream of me?" she said.

Like dust my senses were strewn
across the darkness of the room.
I rose above the stupor of sleep
to answer true from my heart's keep,
"Why invade this dream, so driven,
when for my sin, am I not forgiven?"

"Every night I dream of you,
and of your vengeance, so undue.
I awaken and curse my pain
then sleep to dream of you again.
We danced a dance so incomplete,
cold distance now commands our feet."

I lived a dream never foretold,
filled with a desire uncontrolled,
a two-edged sword of passion's need,
that cut and slashed and made us bleed.
Our stars trembled and held their breath
and watched her stab our love to death.

When the morning completes the night,
I awaken weak, ashen, and contrite
to face the harsh truth of the day,
no escape from the guilt that weighs
like a stone sunk deep in my heart,
a weight that shall never depart.

Humanus Mathematica

The human equation:
a balance of equilibrists
yielding to the manipulations
of relational principles.

The addition of misperceptions
to both sides, are offset
by the subtraction of
irrational doubts.

Multiplication complicates,
adds and amplifies
consequential weight to
both sides of the equation.

Disunity becomes a door,
a portal of escape
from the impossibility
of division by zero.

The calculus of a relationship
is about limits and variables,
seeking integration,
fearing differentiation.

One and one make two,
or so the discipline provides,
but the complexity of life's graph
makes a mockery of the math.

Footprints

When I walk along the beach
with her memory at my side,
I think of possibility's reach
with the rise of the flooding tide.

The cold gray waves slowly sweep
up on time's dark sandy shore,
like a cruel silent thief
stealing all that went before.

Solutions must be kept moist,
issues spread in the sun to dry
lest they empower the choice
to scrawl in the sand, "Goodbye."

The endless sea ends on the shore
in curling, bubbling foam,
leaving untouched her footprints,
sad trail to another's home.

Glass Heart

The sharp sound
of shattering glass
jolted him into reality.

She rudely pranced
past the gold shards
she had just created.

"Please be careful,"
he whispered,
"That is my heart you are breaking."

Then she was gone,
leaving him alone,
to pick up the pieces.

Harsh Words

Harsh words,
arrows of thought,
once released
cannot be recalled.

To their mark
they unerringly fly,
impatient missiles,
sonant messengers of pain.

And so were mine,
shafts of unsanded wood,
feathers from passion's wing,
cruel, reactive points of flinty ego.

Harsh words...
I live and die with mine
and pay the price
for their hurtful sting.

The Road

The road to a lasting love
winds through the valley of regret.
The gypsy in me cannot remember
what is too painful to forget.

John Newlin

Friend and Foe

He was my friend.

We met long ago.

The charm of his boundless promise,
his breadth, enchanted me
and I believed in him.

He was my friend.

With him at my side
the horizon was the edge of eternity,
each day was a wide green pasture,
dotted with bright hued flora
to love and take,
to use and slake,
to bruise and break.

He was my shield
and my narcotic.

He protected me from myself
and he disarmed reality.

He was the promise,
the elusive fountain,
that bubbled and sparkled
under the feckless sun.

He was an enigma,
too profound to comprehend,
like trying to grasp
the relativity of a moonbeam
dancing on one's palm.

I did not look beyond him
nor take daily measure
of the subtle changes
wrought by his constant presence
or the consequences thereof.

Until it was too late.

I awoke from his narcosis
and found that he had become
my enemy.

His presence now is fearsome.
In unvarying tempo,
his hoarse voice whispers
of the urgency
to take one last run

in the diffused light,
through the gray pasture.
for one brief last sip
from the dribbling fountain.

John Newlin

I feel his cold hand in mine,
pulling me steadily toward
the edge of mortality.

He is unrelenting.

Each day he has less to give.

He was once my friend.

He is now my foe.

His name is Time.

Despair

I shall look for her
along the beach,
on wooded trails,
in all the places
we once planned to be...

I committed to forever,
but now it has turned
into endless never.
I could not make the leap
beyond her barb and check.

If I can, I will
put her memory away
into a remote corner
of my heart
where it cannot nourish
my despair.

Maybe

Maybe I've been wrong,
maybe she has been right,
I wonder about that now, since
our time has come and gone.

I loved her walk, it was so perfect,
except when she walked away.

When the fog lifted, she wasn't there...
only moonlight in my hand,
only the miles between
and no hope foreseen.

Maybe my light was too strong,
obscuring her vision;
maybe my voice was too loud,
drowning her song;
maybe my touch was too coarse,
eroding her trust;
maybe my taste was too rich,
threatening her reality;
maybe my scent was too weak
to compete with her roses.

And when I think of her,
I am lost in a sea of unreason
trying to cope with the riot
of so many memories.

She and He

They gazed into their sea, she and he
together as one, each heart to shrink,
shy and reluctant, on the brink,
the edge of loving, which might be,
one outweighing the other, she and he;
each felt their passion rise and sink,
fearing the break of love's fickle link.

On the swells of their divisive sea,
sunlight on the surface, none below,
drowning hearts craving breath for each,
calmly embracing love's slurring speech,
before the sudden ripple in the flow -
two viewed as one vanished beyond reach,
hearts nearly joined, sadly parted so.

John Newlin

The Last Soul Mate

I turned to Love and asked her,
"At long last is this my best day?"
Love's fickle eyes swift averted
as she gave her cold answer, "Nay."

I turned to Hope and beseeched her,
"Do you lurk in Love's cold disdain?"
With a careless shrug Hope replied,
"From all promise I must abstain."

I turned to Faith and pressed her,
"Will her constancy yet hold sway?"
Faith sighed and casually replied,
"Pledges are made to be betrayed."

I turned to Desire and bid her
"Will you the full distance go?"
Desire's soft voice was coldly lent,
"Passion's fire shall yield its glow."

I turned to Loneliness and asked,
"Shall you then be my heart's parole?"
Loneliness took my hand and sighed,
"I'm the last mate of your numb soul."

Sometime

Sometime or other there may be
a face not seen, a voice not heard,
a heart's voice not yet answered,
a whisper of love's promised word.

Sometime or other there might be,
past the horizon's distant sight,
beyond the pain of memories,
sweet silence in the sonant night.

Sometime or other there shall be
a knowing of the thorns that surround
the veinless leaves of a dying year
strewn on the sward, thin and brown.

Sometime or other there must be
the flame upon the flame derived,
leading to the immolation
of a loving heart long deprived.

The Walk

The morning walk knows no fear;
the shadow cast along the way,
preceding each small callow step,
grows short with the hour's decay.

The mid-day walk is burning bright,
no shadow cast to front or rear,
the stride is long, the spirit strong,
fermented in the sun's glare.

The afternoon walk is long and slow,
the trailing shadow tinged with gray.
the ebbing sun is kinder yet
than hazards known along the way.

The evening walk courts the silence
now attending along the road,
and longs anew to wield the strength
an earlier hour once bestowed.

The velvet cloak of darkness falls
and exacts the final toll -
the price of the wondrous walk
Is the surrender of the soul.

The Essence

The essence of life is love,
An extension of the soul
That belies the selfish glove,
On the hand wielding control.

The essence of love is life,
The breathing of vaporous time,
The knowing of unrehearsed strife,
The illusion of hearts sublime.

The essence of pain is doubt,
A lingering ache in the mind
That turns the heart inside out
When faced with truth misaligned.

The essence of doubt is pain,
When taken in a daily dose,
With eyes half-open to the feigned
Images contrived by love's pose.

The essence of essence is hence
One's sense of the sharpened arrow
That pierces one's contrived defense
And bleeds away the heart's marrow.

Schism

One from another,
in body and in mind;
one pledge, two hearts;
amalgamation declined.

One a burden shouldered,
the responsibility applied;
the other a charge rejected,
an obligation denied.

The view from richer ground
is freedom personified;
toiling in twilight's wake
is freedom's loss decried.

Desperate thoughts in words,
within a sad heart conceived,
fail to breach the empty void
and leave only one to grieve.

Years

An ocean of years,
a river of fears,
a lake of tears,
love's debt in arrears.

Waves on a sandy shore,
hearts primed to desire more,
days delighful to explore,
nights to embrace and adore.

Memory's monolith,
reminding not to forget
what we must not regret,
each year's faded vignette.

Elements of our time as one,
sometimes here and sometimes gone,
not yet finished, once begun;
wished never to be undone.

Marionette

A wooden head, a wooden nose,
a wooden shirt and wooden hose,
dancing on the table
parallel strings so apropos.

Painted cheeks and charcoal eyes,
wooden knees, flesh colored dyes,
dancing on the table
a splintered voice badly contrived.

A wooden mind, a wooden soul
a wooden heart on parole,
dancing on the table,
wooden legs deprived of control.

A wooden pyre, a wooden bier,
dark smoke and ashes disappear,
debris on the table -
wooden legacy, flawed and seared.

Her puppetry, cruel animation,
fired his wooden immolation.
Nothing on the table
but his love's desecration.

Dreams

The stuff of dreams was never bought
with rusty coins of inconstant thought
nor with plunder of love distraught.

The stage is set for those who dream
filmy images, entrancing scheme,
islands in reality's stream.

Knowing is day - loving is night.
Phantasms that fail to excite
always dissolve in dawn's cold light.

Dreams that are cloaked in love's attire,
soaked in the sweat of self's desire,
are indulged by elation's choir.

Embrace illusion, not the fact,
sleep in the bed of the abstract,
never admit what might be lacked.

Our dreams are insanity's foe,
where the seeds of fantasia grow
into a new day's hopeful glow.

A Gem

I wear a gem on my finger --
spinel facets glisten in vivid blue,
cradled in golden wings --
from the only jewel I ever knew.

The stone's beauty is forever
the promise of its giving is not --
it was a gift of unpledged love
that time and circumstance forgot.

Treasures

Treasures, carefully collected
from the depths of a smitten mind,
finally put in their rightful place,
so quickly forgotten, left behind.

Unseen photographs torn in half
burning on the pyre of one's fear,
the flames flickering with regret,
evaporating each feckless tear.

Words altered slyly in mid-flight,
cloaked in the sounds of unpledged sighs,
delivered across the senseless void,
on the wings of expectation's demise.

Secrets of frustrated desire lost,
masquerading as passion's needs,
dissolve and fade swiftly away
on the vague surface of love's breeze.

Goodbyes

When we were young
and full of a child's grace,
goodbyes were naively sweet,
their kisses brief and chaste.

Now, with a ripened heart,
farewells are rife with throes,
of sensitive biting thoughts,
like thorns that defend a rose.

Friendship

Your laughter resonates like
a sonorous bell, rich and free,
like the joyful hours spent with you
with which your friendship blesses me.

You are the sweet sound of wind chimes
responding to a vagrant breeze
rising from a sylvan meadow,
alive with shade-giving trees.

I thank you for the things you do,
but even more for what you are;
the spirit of the open sea,
of life's joy beyond the bar.

The Distance

How far the distance
must it be decreed
between she and I
to keep her ever free?

One mile, or two?
or maybe five?
One state, or six,
for love to survive?

How much expanse
must I provide,
to maintain her love
vibrant and alive?

One room, or two?
Three canyons away?
Hope for a virtual hug
languishing every day?

How many arid weeks
must creep slowly past
before each new sip
from love's distant glass.

How much is enough
to refill my heart,
following the days
and nights far apart.

Too much is not enough,
of her for me.
thus the sad truth
seems ever to be;

too many long miles,
too many deep sighs,
too many soft hellos,
too many hard goodbyes.

Too many ups and downs
along the distant way;
too much barb and check
denying love's sway.

John Newlin

Her Memory

I slowly awaken in the midst of night
and feel my dreams of her melt away.
then I surface in the morning light
and look where once her body lay.

But I did not find her there asleep,
just her memory lies in that space,
where once I swam in a rapture deep,
but now find emptiness in its place.

No bare back next to me
no sound of breath's sweet bliss,
nothing there for me to see,
nor bare shoulder to receive a kiss.

To Forget

I know not from whence came the wine
that she had given me to drink;
since my first taste I have forgotten
all the deep things I used to think.

Last night I went into the fields
and asked of the gods there: 'Pray,
which herb might be a cure for love?'
But the gods refused to say.

She led me up a narrow slope,
up to the shining hill above;
and there she cruelly showed me
the way to forget how to love.

Sad is the solemn fate of those
who never loved, spring or fall;
but to love and then to forget,
that is the saddest fate of all.

John Newlin

Our First Christmas

Here is wishing that this Christmas shall be
the first of many for us yet to come,
finding great happiness beneath the tree,
wrapped in the tissue of our love's sum.

Our years melt into a timeless river.
like dwindling islands in the stream,
we erode more than we would deliver,
but not the expectation of our dreams.

Yet love is the mirror of forever,
bold and inspiring to the tearless eye,
whose image of our coming together
is more enduring than the reason why.

So take my hand this joyous Christmas day
and let our remaining days be as bright,
so that someday we can look back and say,
each became the other's warm Yule light.

The Poem I Wish She Had Written

Not in my wildest dreams did I believe
that I would ever be so in love with you,
that my fear of love could ever be relieved
nor the splendor of its bliss I would construe.

Then, in the gulf between flight and pleasure,
caged by the freedom of myself alone,
deep within my heart I beheld a treasure
of greater worth than any I had known.

The love I feared has arrived undaunted,
leaving me conflicted and out of breath,
but the need for your love leaves me haunted,
trembling, joyful, mesmerized by it's depth.

Your love for me I cannot reject,
my love for you has so impassioned me,
beguiled me to take down the barb and check
and let the beauty of your heart set me free.

John Newlin

Garden of Love

As the road grows shorter,
And the day latens and wanes,
My thoughts turn to her beauty
And the place where serenity reigns.

I'm weary from climbing the mountain,
Of scaling the cliffs high above,
Now that dusk is upon me,
I seek to rest in her garden of love.

Thanksgiving

When the special meal was finished,
when the silver was put away,
I bowed my head in special thanks
That she was with me on that day.

A Poem Not Written

He tried to write a poem
about his soul's demise;
of waking in an empty bed,
uncaring in the depth of night,
of the numbness in his heart,
of the flame inside that was dead.

Then she stepped in through time's door,
and carressed the hands she once loved,
and in the midst of a moonlit night
began to fill his vacant soul
with the vibrancy of her love,
quelling the verse he would not write.

John Newlin

I Could Forget

I could forget
a summer breeze,
gently rustling blossoms in a field,
but not her name.

I could forget
a dying sun painting
the rim of the earth in scarlet,
but not her lips.

I could forget
the silver cusp of a half moon
reflected in the lambent surface of a lake,
but not her eyes.

I could forget
the sweet melodious trill
of a lark in full-throated ecstasy,
but not her voice.

I could forget
all the joys that have
embellished my life...
but never her.

Alone

I am alone tonight
and yet my spirit sings
softly in the darkness
of the tranquility that you bring.

I am alone tonight
and yet my heart smiles
tenderly in the darkness
at the dissolving of our miles.

I am alone tonight
and yet my love glows
brightly in the darkness
ignited by what it knows.

Loneliness was once a pain
I knew every dark night,
that has been banished
by the warmth of love's light.

John Newlin

Coffee

Coffee - stimulant or depressant, we
turn to the aroma at the day's start,
and relish the flavor from dark liquid
whose hot temper excites the waking heart.

We - you and I - have tasted from the cup
and sallied forth into the waiting day,
our senses heightened and sharpened to cope
with all the joys and strains along our way.

But nothing can so easily compare
to the joy of sipping from the hot brew
of liquid love that follows the short night,
a sip which we shall never bid adieu.

Time

Time is a river, but I dare not know
which way it wends or its rate of flow,
or in which guise it might currently be robed,
nor can its depths be accurately probed.

I am an island in time's midstream,
a waveless, shoreless, directionless dream.
as the current flows too swift to withstand,
each precious day becomes a grain of sand

hurling downward through the neck of time's glass,
measuring the future but not the past.
each moment of time, a drop of love's demand,
vaporized in loneliness's cold hand.

John Newlin

A Spinster

In the cold remembrance
of unrequited thought,
taunting like an old maid's
twittering song overwrought,

a lover might conclude
that a wing and a prayer
are insincere partners
in surviving thin air,

and trust and investment
in a spinster's shrewd art
shall thus surely result
in a hole in one's heart.

Things Unsaid

When one takes up the pen and writes his love,
he must be mindful to be discrete,
and choose his verse with exacting care
lest his words she should in the future repeat.

One must remember and never forget
that each love letter's content is long lived;
the precious recipient will put them away
for later retrieval from her archive.

And then woe to the lover, whose writings
reveal himself at a moment of life's time,
giving her a window through which to peer
back into the depths of his bare soul's prime.

If she seeks reasons to mistrust his love,
she will reach into her private store of him
and dwell and concentrate on every word
that that gives rise to her every doubting whim.

So every man who feels the need to write
sweet everlasting words of love sore bled,
beware her need to carefully preserve
all those things you might regret you said.

John Newlin

A Mother's Lament (For Pat)

Perhaps I need to drift.

She has sailed on upon
a sudden autumn leaf
to waver above the earth,
flying in uncharted direction,
upward and round the bend of time
waiting there for me.

The crush, the resounding grief,
wading deep into her memory,
coping with fate's cruel dust,
thrown into a mother's eyes
by an uproarious wind.

Perhaps I should weep now
and wind down from the coil
of breathless pain,
always knowing,
but never understanding
why she had to leave.

Each tomorrow is punishing
but it is life - I need to accept it.

Should I navigate each turn
with keen intent and direction,
so that I twist away from the whirlwind
of passing through the echoes
of her life?

Will I ride this autumn nightmare
with metered cadence
or a slow unsteady wobble?

Or may I, oh please god, just drift!

The Look of Her

He touched her hand
as they listened
to the sounds of the snow
softening the ground.

He wanted to tell her
how he had come to be,
what he was...

About his life, about the world,
the way of him, in the cold,
under the icey dogwood petals,
the way his love had taken wing.

She listened but did not heed.

Like leaves vibrating
in the cold wind,
a panic shivered within him.

At that awful moment
he knew that she would go.

And she did.

Redemption

If you should think ill of him,
and flay him with words so cold,
perhaps it would be fairer still
to know which essence to behold;

For has he not lived two lives?
And suffered long the first
and only recently did know
your judgment need be reversed?

So cast aspersions if you must,
upon his reckless heart of old,
but be kind and leave unscathed
his redemptive soul.

John Newlin

Mystery

I would write a poem
and send it on to thee
could I find nouns and verbs
that explain the mystery

of red feathered arrows,
flying to intended mark;
of narcotic music
mesmerizing the dark;

of importuning doves
each bearing a thornless rose,
of giddy walks a'reeling,
from sultry desire exposed;

of diaphanous dreams,
hypnotic visions nigh,
nightly perspiration,
yearning's effort doth supply;

But the muse avoids me,
words flee this smitten mind,
therefore all that is sent
Is my love -- unrefined.

The Crystal Spider

Take me with you everywhere
so that you will always know
that the one who gave me to you
loves you and loves your soul.

And as the years melt away
remember this all else above;
my sparkling beauty, crystal clear,
pales in the glow of his vibrant love.

Tightrope

A step - cautious, tentative
along the high wire;
place each trembling foot
ahead of the other - slowly.

How high is too high?
How long the fall?
One slip, one mistake
and you will know.

Balance is everything.
a precarious journey
for older weary legs
struggling for equilibrium.

The wire sways in the wind.
How much breeze is too much?
Counterpoise the zephyr
or take the last flight.

Do not look down,
no turning back.
The terminus is shrouded
in misty uncertainty.

Sway with the wire,
find the rhythm,
or the dissonance
will tip the balance.

Let go of the fear
if you can - let it go
or it will embrace you
and drop with you like a stone.

How many steps remain?
How many are too many?
There may be only one.
The next and the last one.

John Newlin

A New Day

I dream of you in the cool night,
something I sometimes fear to do;
to walk with you so silently
through past adventures that we knew.

Our steps orchestrate old feelings,
the strident unrequited strings,
the winds exhaling passion's sighs,
percussive echos of love's stings.

I dance with desire a thousand times,
not knowing it is you in disquise,
and ignore the music playing,
never dreaming of its demise.

But just before awakening,
the greeting of the new day's dawn,
I lead you onto a fairer path
that promises the light beyond.

I call to you and sofly say,
come join me in my new found sun,
it's time to leave this dream behind,
our glorious new day has begun.

Pearls

Our days are like a string of pearls,
each lustrous gem strung by hand,
nature's imperfect beauty
conceived around a grain of sand.

A grain a day through narrow glass,
time's gift to each loving heart,
a pearl in the string of memories,
a gleaming necklace of life's art.

And as the string grows longer still,
each by each a day's story tells
of wondrous findings in our world
and better knowing of ourselves.

Her Voices

She walked among the flowers,
under the early morning sun,
her misty thoughts were of him,
her heart in hand and not yet won.

Voices drifted to her from the foliage
of her life's wending verdant way,
from dearest angels to impart
their advice, trust them as she may.

Voices like bells chiming in her head,
distinct notes of romantic day,
urging her, as one, to go forward
and embrace love's final way.

But still she paused and looked back
down the longest road traveled
and reflected a little sadly
on how desire came unraveled.

Yet one melodic voice spoke to her
of the path that lay ahead,
to softly, gently persuade her
to unbend and let go all her dread.

His harmony was so heady
and filled with such compelling art,
that she felt herself loosening
the grip of the hand that held her heart.

Each new song weakened and touched her
and left its indelible brand.
Would she yield to all his wooing
and extend to him her heart in hand?

The Dilemma

She drank deeply from love's cup
and reeled from the heady brew
surprised to be an inebriate,
stunned by feelings she could not subdue.

His fingers played upon her keys
making music not known before,
a steady, throbbing cadence,
drumming at her heart's locked door.

And deep within her inner self
she sighed for harmony's emotion
and longed to bathe once again
in the dew of old devotions.

But high above in virgin tower,
a clarion call sounded clear
to marshal her defenses,
to shield her independence dear.

A bolt and bar at every door,
no window left unguarded,
and afterglow's sweet effect
painfully disregarded.

Yet she sipped - and sipped again,
from his deep well of desire,
subverting her cool resolve
not to accept and don love's attire.

An aversion as old and as strong
as her baptismal sacrament,
to love's unspoken demand
they be coupled by commitment.

Can we keep the music playing?
Can we sustain the romance?
Can we ever choreograph
the give and take of love's dance?

And so she spun 'round and 'round
in ambivalent extremis,
turning oft to Libra's scales,
to weigh and measure her dilemma.

But the freedom of space and time
says so much a precious gem
that it weighed ever heavily
against the presence of him.

When the image of him refused
to melt and silently depart
her dilemma deepened and
tormented her divided heart.

Her mind became a pendulum,
defining her role in their drama:
knowing her struggle impaled him
on the horns of her dilemma.

John Newlin

His love bled so profusely
from the wounds so deeply riven
that it paled and weakly died
from her dilemma, so blindly driven.

A Whisper

A whisper.
Words cloaked in a hushed voice;
softly uttered thoughts floating
like feathers floating on a zephyr.

A whisper.
Secret knowings, private words
slipping through trusting lips
into a confidant's ear.

A whisper.
The wind teasing the tree tops
on cat-like feet, unseen, unheard,
barely rustling the surprised leaves.

A whisper.
A lover's words sweetly breathed
through cotton candy lips,
melting in her waiting ear.

A whisper.
The rusty sigh of welcome
to the dearest love raised from
the enduring shadows of yesteryear.

A whisper.
By the cold breath of farewell
to a guiltless soul gone astray,
such a thankless soul did betray.

Friendship And Wine

From the grape comes the wine
that will so enchant our lips,
and stimulate our palate
with every precious sip.

When the last of this wine
has been poured, red and dry,
our friendship shall endure
far beyond our next good-bye.

Fear

If you are afraid to love,
then I am so alone.
If you are afraid to give,
then I am an unknown.
If you are afraid of your heart,
then I am a soul undone.
If you are afraid of my heart,
then darkness cloaks the sun.

Discovery

I saw you with my eyes, but not my mind.
I touched you with my hands, but not my heart.
I laughed with you with my lips, but not my soul.
I gave you my body, but not my love.

And now...

My mind sees you.
My heart touches you.
My soul laughs with yours.
My body loves you.

There is nothing more wondrous than to be
a man who is discovering himself.

John Newlin

Memories

Memories are
much like dreams.

So elusive
in their quicksilver readiness
to slide away from us
just when we think
we can grasp them.

Two Hearts

A single flame,
bright and pure,
burning in two hearts,
love's ardent signature.

A single thought,
intense desire,
invading two minds
that with love conspire.

A single song,
a ballad sweet,
rising from two throats,
love's melody elite.

A single night,
a wondrous reunion
fusing two souls
via love's communion.

Saving The Tiger

There once was an old tiger
who lived in a self-made cage
whose only strong emotion
was occasional, irrational rage.

The old feline had lost his spirit
and languished in his hole.
He had pined away his mettle
and abandoned his empty soul.

Nothing seemed to move him,
he knew no light, no heat.
He turned his back on the future;
he had surrendered to defeat.

Then, from out of his past
there emerged a living flame,
a bright-eyed, graceful figure
who drove away his shame.

She whispered of the future
and challenged him to gauge
the real and imagined limits
of the boundaries of his cage.

Vivified and emboldened
the old one uttered a growl
and from his cage unfettered
he began a fearless prowl.

He leapt and pranced and roared
as he pawed each new gem;
all the world's sweet wonders
were opening up to him.

Now the tiger's tawny body
is lithe and fierce and alive
and the essential essence
of his soul has been revived.

John Newlin

Numbers

Dissolution is all about the numbers,
not about the demise of love,
nor the loss of respect,
nor failure to understand,
nor the need to molt and move aside.

It's all about the numbers.
How much property to cleave in two:
the house, cars, bank accounts?
Silver, jewels, bedroom suite?
A number is essential to divide.

Numbers rule.
Support for each month,
insurance, care for health,
food, clothing, rent,
a number determined to provide.

No wringing of hands,
nor beating of breast,
nor woeful cries of wrecked union.
only the numbers mutely stand
to witness drowning in the tide.

If Love Is To Be

If love is to be as indelible
as a promise written in heart's blood,
if it is to be made as enduring
as all of love's dreams imbued,

If love is to be as resilient
as the supplest willow tree,
if it is to be as true and trustful
as the comfort of a mother's knee,

If love is to be as fresh and candid
as an unposed photograph,
if it is to grow and flourish
like the blades of sweet spring grass,

Then each partner must inter their doubts
and trust the clarity of the lover's sight,
and cherish the awesome feeling
of the other's love close by each night.

One Night With Venus

She was an ebony temptress
with long lovely legs spread wide
across the glistening array
of threads spun from her finest silk.
woven to lure, capture, and dine
on each unwary male roue.

Each sunny morning diamond drops
of shimmering dew bedecked
the thin strands of her filmy nest
like sparkling alluring beacons
signaling safe sexual congress
to her unsuspecting guests.

The morning zephyr teased the glade
and gently strummed her silken strands
like the strings of aphrodite's lyre
wafting a song of seduction
through the boughs of the leafy glen
setting prey's lusty hearts afire.

On came her suitors, one by one
drawn to her diaphanous lair,
sensual love at last to debut,
never heeding nature's warning
etched brightly on her black belly -
a red hourglass-shaped tattoo.

And each lusty, virile male
danced to the center of her web
to mount her body and remain
with her in a final clutching throe,
excruciating carnal pleasure
alloyed with endless pain.

Weak, with love's strength sapped,
the victim lay silent, prostrate
on her ethereal bed,
his magnificent black body
now a desiccated shell
sucked dry and dead.

It was his ill-fated lot
to fill her body with his seed,
to propagate their species
and fill her with a living brood,
all for the terrible price
of his one night with Venus.

Soul Lover

"I love your soul," she whispered
from the distance of night and day.
Can such a one love my soul
and not love me in the same way?

Can she be so enamored of
the soulful nature of me
that she looks past the heart
that conducts soul's symphony?

And if she does, then does it mean
that her love be less than fair,
giving cause for fear and worry
that loving her might reap despair?

Sadly, I know the kind of love
that weakens and begins to pale,
after conquering that part of me
where none other has prevailed.

The Poet's Gift

> To some the art is given,
> insights received from heaven.
> The muse shall then enfold
> in each the fabric of her soul.

Cassius Crow

Cassius Crow was a big old bird
with shiny feathers, long and black.
his family members, near and dear
jawed at each other - clackity clack.

Cassius' flock nested in a wood
full of pine from old Monterey
and as far as old Cassius knew
they'd dwelt there forever and a day.

He and his kin loved to launch
and mount the unbounded sky,
wheeling and swooping and soaring,
tail chasing in full throated cry.

Up and up they would gaily flap,
climbing the steep ladder of the sky,
then tightly fold their satin wings
and drop like a stone in a dive.

'Round and 'round in the firmament
they would cavort far above the sward
while all around the periphery
uncles and cousins stood the guard.

Once a sassy little Jay bird
began reciting verse from Poe,
Cassius snidely croaked his retort,
"You don't know a raven from a crow."

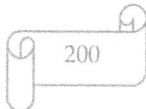

And in the spring when Robin came
Hippity hopping around the flock,
And acting like his poop didn't stink,
Cassius gibed, "Crows don't hop. We walk."

They would gobble up all the grain,
melons and eggs and most the rest,
but their sharp-eyed hunger also claimed
grasshoppers, worms, and lots of pests.

Cassius Crow was a sanguine bird
that always knew the score,
the one word he would never croak
was the ill-fated "Nevermore."

Love and He

He: "Who are you?"

Love: "I am love."

He: "What are you."

Love: "I am the self-portrait
of anyone brave enough
to make a gift of me
to another."

He: "But I don't have you.
How can I give
what I don't have?"

Love: "That's my paradox.
You cannot have me
until you give me."

He: "But it makes no sense.
And why brave?"

Love: "It takes courage
to conquer the fear
of not having me."

He: "I'm lost.
When will I be found?"

Love: "When you can give me
to one who may not want me."

The Old Tiger

A raunchy old tiger lay in his lair
Dreaming and drooling over a tigress fair.

Her yellow eyes searching, a flash in the night
Seeking her prey, so swift to take flight.

Her sleek haunches rippling in her tense crouch,
Her white fangs gleaming from her hungry mouth.

Her lovely lips curled in a vicious snarl,
Her pointy ears alert for unseen peril.

The sly, creeping style of her nightly stalk,
The sensual sashay of her killer walk.

Her sinuous tail twitching left and then right
As she feeds in epicurean delight.

The old cat purred and rolled onto his back,
Smitten by the vision in orange and black.

She was his dream, savagely sweet feline,
On whose striped back he longed to recline.

And so to woo her and her love recruit
He bought her a box of JujyFruit.

Someday

Someday when we are more than gray
and are sitting by a dying fire
I'll take your hand in mine and recall
the breadth and depth of our desire.

I'll look deep into your dark eyes,
and reach out to touch your soft cheek,
and think how much we would have missed
had this love been beyond our reach.

I'll pull you near for a tender hug,
to feel your heart beating with mine
and remember that wondrous night
when we loved and talked and sipped the wine.

The wine that aged as many days
as had passed since we first did love,
had been waiting through all those years
to celebrate our passion's trove.

I'll press my lips to your cool brow
and whisper ever so softly to you
how we carved from our latter years
a monument to our love so true.

Sweet Soul Mate

Oh sweet soul mate, once love of mine,
who now I cannot touch nor see,
I know you no more for me pine,
yet shall bide in yon shadow's lee.

Once your eyes blazed end to trouble,
once you lips curled sweet with mirth,
once we knew our pleasure double
before I knew that treasure's worth.

And sweet soul mate I remember
the sorest of those bygone years
when you left in cold December
with sad dark eyes devoid of tears.

Separate paths have been traveled
by, sweet soul mate, you and I
and even though we came unraveled
our soul's thread never lost the tie.

But now, sweet soul mate, we both wait
for the dark drawing of the shade.
The consummation of our fate
awaits us in a distant glade.

So, sweet soul mate, while yet dreaming
ethereal dreams by the sea,
abandon lonely thoughts unseeming--
the soul in you is yet shared by me.

A Poem

I think
there is nothing
that would improve my day
more than writing a poem
for you.

A verse or two
of scintillating rhyme,
or perhaps just some
lambent prose, to enchant
or amuse.

A gift not to refuse,
nor to put quickly aside
but to read again and again
through the years
that might accrue,
crippling phantasm
that confounds unsated souls.

John Newlin

Risk

The waters are dark
and so bitter cold,
the ice is thin -
dare not be bold.

The trap is subtle,
and in the deep pit,
waiting sharpened stakes -
dare not to commit.

Pain is a serpent,
coiled in silent wait
to strike at the heart -
dare not tempt your fate.

Poise is well balanced
above the harsh squall,
humiliation looms below -
dare not risk the fall.

Hold gold and silver
in your sweaty palm,
the future's a gamble -
dare you be undone.

The face of risk
daunts the timid heart
of the one afraid -
daring not to take part.

Another Dream

Somewhere in the night I hear her singing,
in a voice too alluring to repel
and the melody, so sweetly stinging,
unravels my slumber and breaks its spell.

Her song arrives on the crest of a breeze
from the horizon beyond my sleep,
softly chanting a harmonic reprise,
striking a chord deep in my heart's keep.

I labor to attend it and harken close
by every note of that divine refrain,
its melancholy lyrics expose
a haunting trace of love's previous reign.

'Tis a loving voice, one I once did know;
a dulcet voice and pure as summer rain,
calling me, bidding me to rise and go,
to lie with her and taste her love again.

I rise trembling and to the window stride
to throw open wide the window glass
and exult in my heartfelt, yearning cry,
pledging to her my love unsurpassed.

Then her song softens, begins melting down
like mountain snow into a cool, still stream,
and I, swaddled in damp sheets around,
awaken yet from a another dream.

John Newlin

My Father

"Go now, my young warrior."
my father's voice was proud.
"Go and learn to fly and sing.
Go and learn that man is not God."

His joy burst through his grin
as he watched me walking tall
into the future's fickle grasp,
never looking back at all.

But before I left there was wisdom
to impart--knowledge to give to me.
"Returning without your shield is
better than upon it", said he.

"If you confuse pride with honor
and count success as victory,
you shall not know the peace
of maturing gracefully.

You shall be beset by enemies,
in your travels far and wide.
But the greatest peril lies
Within you, where your self resides.

You must acquaint yourself with fear,
and know well its numbing tide,
but never allow it to reign
in place of judgment's guide.

Your shield surely will be pierced,
but not from arrow or lance.
The main assault will come
from love's immobilizing trance.

When you have supped at the table
of humility and disgrace,
then shall you know full the measure
of the courage hiding in your breast.

Know well, my son, that life's
deepest and most painful wounds
are not given to the flesh,
but to the soul's fragile bloom.

Deliver no harm to others,
although they may give such to you.
Vengeance is a strong temptation,
but do not collect the piper's due.

You are of my flesh and blood,
yet you share not my destiny,
that you have your own to shape
is your most precious legacy."

These words, never spoken,
were of immeasurable worth.
He died the day I left, but his
gifts have been mine since birth.

John Newlin

Old Friend

Well, old friend, the gate hinge
is creaky and caked with rust
from too many selfish tears
embedded in the crust.

Try the gate, if you will,
old friend, but I do doubt
it shall yield to your touch
and let the bitter out.

And the well, old friend, now
echoes from stony depths;
the emptiness therein
hastened by greedy lips.

Let down the pail, old friend,
and expect then the worst
of finding you must go
elsewhere to slake your thirst.

And the windows, old friend,
are grimy, sooty panes
unwashed by caring hands
nor baptized by the rains.

Peer, old friend, if you can
into that murky room.
The warm glow of past brilliance
is replaced by haunting gloom.

The gate, well, and glass, old friend,
once so new, deep, and bright,
are rusty, dry, and dim
in today's failing light.

Thus, old friend, the decay
has exacted its hoary toll
and laid its heavy hand
upon this jaded soul.

John Newlin

The Day

The day is not yet over,
though distant is the cool dawn.
Bruises earned in morning's heat
are faded and pale—almost gone.

Scars from mid-day battle
tattoo an hide.
Blurry afternoon vision
discerns the evening tide.

Is there time before nightfall
to search along the way
for the mystery of love
to crown this long, hard day?

Love's Labor

Does she complain that her depth exceeds
the modest length of your dearest deeds?
Does she conspire to whisper rank and low,
that your most wanton rhythm is too slow?

Does she protest that your erudition
is more agile than sublime position?
Does she denounce with vitriolic spice
your laying down so soon the sweetest price?

Does she decry with bitter, angry prose
your swift descent into deep repose?
If she does, give her this thought to savor:
love's noble pleasure loses its flavor
when thus sentenced to suffer hard labor.

A Question

Is the nectar
of anticipation sweeter
than the wine distilled
from tomorrow turned yesterday?

Is the tender moment
of profound release
sustaining enough to bridge
the emptiness left in its wake?

Is a song unsung
wilting on mute lips
sadder than the banked fires
fading in tearless eyes?

Is the coming of rain
to an arid heart
more fearful than the rage
of the tempest bearing it?

To Tell A Love

How does one tell of one love to another?
In voice quicker and drier than the wind,
pretending the cup shared with the former
quenched no thirst from its imperfect blend?

How does one recount to one's current love
the loving once so fervently embraced?
With glib tongue and averted eyes above,
no hint that old thoughts ever be retraced?

How, to a now love, does one ever speak
of the gladdened days and nights freely spent
basking in the warm glow of former fire's heat?
With feckless words of disdain, coldly lent?

How, to a true love, does one yet express
an older love's truth not yet forgotten?
With cotton candy lips so sweetly pressed
on melting words deceitfully begotten?

How does one say of an old love to new?
By holding new love so tenderly near.
By speaking of love's worth, so dear, so true
and no word of old love finding new's ear.

John Newlin

Once I Knew Thee

Once I knew thee well,
once thee did know me,
but fate's cold whim
wrought our delirium
casting each adrift in a different sea.

Knowing is thy guilt,
caring shall be mine.
The stars dare not know
from whence came their glow,
nor in whose dark night they shine.

Rivers flood their banks,
flowers shed their bloom.
yearning is painful,
denial more gainful
than a dead love one day exhumed.

Sad it seems to me
our lives be so diverse.
mine so defenseless,
thine so relentless,
and just one soul to know remorse.

Thus it may be true,
the gulf is far too wide.
I shall forgive thee,
lest thee outlive me
and whisper my name to the ebbing tide.

Thy Beauty

Thy beauty is to me
as profound as the sea,
as thorny as the rose
that in pain's garden grows,
as awesome as the sun
feigning death when day is done,
as diamond studded bright
as cold and cloudless night.

Thy passion is to me
as deep rooted as a tree,
as potent as the flame
that immolates my shame,
as eloquent as the verse
with which the poet bursts,
as wholesome as the grain
kissed sweet by heaven's rain.

Thy going is to me
as bitter as the sea,
as arid as the sand
creeping over the desert land,
as numbing as the cold
that blows from winter's fold,
as final as the death
of love's last sweet breath.

John Newlin

The Drifter

Patiently twilight and I
await the languid sinking
of a copper stained sun
from the graying sky
marbled with blue.

The pallid dusk
will soon cloak the land
with melting shadows
blurring and fading to the sound
of my sighing.

Like a fragile tumbleweed
I will ride the night wind
away from this domain
leaving old dreams to dissolve
in the morning sun.

The fresh dawn
will find me in a new land
giving birth to new dreams,
new desires, in brief respite
from troubled journey.

But the new
shall become the old
and twilight's muted voice
will summon the restless night wind
and I will leave my dreams again.

Come Back Moses

Come back Moses, from yesteryear,
and do my bidding once again.
Go thee down and plumb the sorrow
embedded in the hearts of men.

See the caverns in their eyes,
their steel and glass alluring,
taste the bile of their rejection,
mark their idols, yet enduring.

Hark their glib words from pulpits flowing,
hear their mendacities coldly lent.
read the irony in their gospel,
breathe the maelstrom of their discontent.

Ancient servant and voice of mine,
I gave thee once a scripted stone
and sent thee down the mountainside
to guide them near to heaven's throne,

Since, Moses, that millennium
woefully have I sunk to dwell
into the darkness of Acheron --
the love of man has been my hell.

It is whispered Moses, among men,
that God is dead -- it is no lie.
Go thee down now and say this truth:
out of pity for man did I die.

John Newlin

Night Launch

At sea the moonless, mantled night
is blacker than a hundred midnights
deep in the maw of a cypress swamp
and the aircraft carrier's deck lights
are hooded and dimly impotent.

Sixty feet above the sea's foaming curl
sleek swept-winged birds are unchained
from the slippery gray steel flight deck.
The sound of hot, howling engines
scream their power to sustain flight.

The inky blackness is punctuated
by director's glowing amber wands,
like syncopated fireflies
beaconing signals by practiced hands,
guiding blind craft to the catapult.

The movement is a symphony
of frantic, chaotic precision
that reaches a shuddering crescendo
with each taut, measured decision
to unleash the catapult's awesome might.

Each cockpit is an instrumented
womb of pale red profusion,
eerily silhouetting mask and helmet
donned by young lions--their calm tension
mounting as the critical moment nears.

First a red wand circles, stabs the gloom,
urging throttles forward to ignite
twin afterburner tongues of flame
searing the fragile veil of the night.
The tethered bird shrieks and strains to soar.

Then the green wand--all is right--
signals in a graceful, swinging arc.
powerful scalding, steam is unleashed
to hurl the bird into the milky dark,
jolting the pilot with blurring force.

And the loud, sweaty ballet goes on
as each winged chariot, one by one,
is given the wrenching gift of flight,
until the last is away and gone,
engines' thunder fading in the night.

John Newlin

The Sea

The sea, wide and blue,
does not reveal all that's in her
but bears me silently,
bears me tenderly
and surrenders only to the wind
of my passion, my desire.

My wake divides her unchaste surface,
a narrow incision
churning in frothy profusion
across her billowed breast;
then fading, it perishes
in the vastness of her restless flux.

Briefly the shadow of my wings
darkens her foam-crested mantle
as it heaves restlessly,
mirroring the wheeling, soaring migration
of my untethered soul.

At voyage's end
when the dying tempest shrieks no more,
in her bosom the memory lingers
and she shall harbor
my secret illusions
sunk in her depths like a stone.

Voices

The voices from the canyon,
in dissonant chirping whirring chorus,
were sweet contradiction of
the stubborn disquieting suspicions
lurking in the silence of her mind.

But doubt became a partner of time
when a smart cocking of her head
was no longer enough
to focus on the jello voices
blending into vague profusion.

Bewilderment then surrendered to fear
as inflections so easily slipped
from her aural grasp
and softly uttered words
died mysteriously in mid-flight.

Taking dark reality by the hand,
she unsheathed her courage
and lifting up her firm chin
made an unwelcome corner in her life
for the permanence of her affliction.

Twin accomplices now attend her,
miniature extensions of her damaged sense
that return to her some clarity
of nouns and verbs and all the things
so vital to her listening.

John Newlin

Helen

The face that launched
a thousand ships
smiled at me across the years.

Dark brilliant eyes
and perfect lips
reflecting in a hundred mirrors.

Her poise, her grace,
her Grecian brow,
invaded my unguarded mind.

Lithe supple frame
so near somehow,
more intoxicating than the wine.

Ancient beauty--
yet so young,
a glint of fervor's pulsing glow?

Sweet liquid love,
from olive wrung,
forbidden fruit I dare not know.

This wine is too ripe
to suit the blend,
her heart lies beyond my zeal,

yet fair Helen
shall be sweet friend
and ever my Achilles heel.

Death's Claim

When Death claims the body,
the pale unwelcome guest
untethers the living soul,
renders flesh and bone into dust.

The body's mortal suffering
is swiftly melted down
and, like the body's blood,
dissolves in Death's cold hand.

The spirit soars and sings,
the senses embrace the bliss.
The heart, its task ended,
sublimes away to nothingness.

When death claims the spirit,
ignoring the reeling mind,
the soul is a prisoner
of its fickleness refined.

Flesh hangs limp on the bone;
bone aches more than the flesh.
The senses slowly drown
in a river of emptiness.

The spirit sags and kneels
under its own leaden weight.
Mortal suffering seems endless.
the heart is disconsolate.

Alas Dear Madam

Alas, dear Madam, have I thee wronged
by gesture, savage word, or deed,
thus giving thee cause for sorrow
importuning your heart to bleed?

Have I, dear Madam, given thee
injury so rank and so low
as to merit your cool design
to suffer me the status quo?

Dear Madam, have I deceived thee
and showered thee with silken lies,
or primed thee with honeyed words
to cloak dark purpose in disguise?

Nay, dear Madam, no wrong to thee
did I meanly perpetrate.
no grievous sin did I commit,
nor cold insult dedicate.

My grossest error, dear Madam,
was to unknowingly explore
the pride sleeping in your bosom
and its delicacy ignore.

So, dear Madam, please forgive me
for the numb bruises I once gave
to that one part of a woman
which no man should ever brave.

John Newlin

The River

The river sings its sweet lament
in ancient voice softly lowing,
vibrant melodies subtly meant
to plumb the depths of our knowing.

Around each bend it curves, flowing
onward toward its fated reunion
with unkempt sea, wild and blowing;
embraced in briny communion.

Its serpentine course scars the land
in undulant brown profusion;
shimmering gold in twilight's hand,
a gift of nature's effusion.

Pregnant spring plies it, unleashing
tempest's turgid downpour to slake
the lusty spate's thirst unceasing,
leaving ravaged marl in its wake.

Torrid summer's breath chars the soil
and saps the river of its strength,
but cool and sweet, the river's toil
paints a green ribbon down its length.

Demon winter glazes the earth,
garbs the river in frigid gown,
draws a pane of ice over its girth
but fails to stay its flowing down.

Since time out of mind, the river
has carved canyons from stubborn stone
and sought naught but to deliver
its lifeblood back to heaven's home.

John Newlin

Southeast of April

Southeast of April lies a land
wherein my heart is sweetly shaped
and quintessential serenity
is upon my soul's shoulders draped.

There riant laughter rides the wind
like a crisp autumnal leaf
tumbling down the honeyed air
over the canyon's dark relief.

There my sorrows, like crystal drops
of dew, dissolve in the swift sun,
and the sonority of twilight
serenades my gentle sleep begun.

No furious gales there do blow,
no savage storms of need and lust
nor rage of unrequited desire
disturbs my soul's somnific dust.

Nor does rabid howl of anger
reverberate throughout this land,
nor does the dog of self pity
come whining at my command.

Nothing but this land's sorbent veil
can quell my spirit's harsh riot,
smother my heart's selfish craving
and soothe my wretched disquiet.

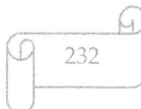

Where is this land of which I laud?
Southeast of April it does lie,
where one may not easily go--
least of all one so mortal as I.

John Newlin

The Resurrection

He that seeks gazes with solemn eye
upon himself as he would a love,
and in loving hard does despise
what he treasures none else above.

It is in that loneliness of love
of himself that his creation
rings with laughter, crystal pure,
an echo of his salvation.

In the cold breath of solitude
is born the fear of the lonely.
There he must vie like a lover
to find his love, one and only.

All your loneliness is but guilt,
it is said in contradiction
of the agony deep in he
who confronts his own affliction.

Solitude and pride are old foes,
their struggle shall make him weary;
who braves the ghostly passage
through himself, leaden and teary.

He must know the pain of dying
and his whole heart it must consume.
There can be no resurrection
without descent into the tomb.

Her Silence

Her silence fell, a leaden pall
across the lonely, barren hours;
insouciant gift of bitter gall
wilting the plush and verdant flowers.

Blossoms fair of need that flourished
in the inner garden, fervent
with concord, budding and nourished
with hope faith would be our servant.

Yet was the cold stillness unveiled
and our amity thus invaded,
until newfound thirst prevailed
and came humble upon wings belated.

Too late, too late, selfish lady,
give it no more that a fleeting thought.
harmony's wine is far too heady
for you ever to quench the drought.

John Newlin

Could I But Know

Could I but know
The gilded glow
Of sparkling cloud and spire;
Could I but dwell
Within the knell
Of the fame that all desire.

Could I but bye
And softly lie
In love's sweetly scented bower,
Or bravely roam
Through silent gloam
To grasp and wield her power.

But I have knelt
And bear the welt
Of the stinging lash of sorrow;
For by my deed
And fate's fickle need,
Six have lost their morrow.

And I stood alone,
Heard no groan
Of lament from her mute lips;
No missives bright
To cure the blight
Came nigh from her fingertips.

And the loyal oak,
When tested, broke
And offered not its haven
From the stinging rain
Of blinding pain
and mocking cries from the raven.

Could I not tell
The way to hell
And wherein lies its burning?
For fate's cold blade
Has cruelly flayed
The flesh from off my yearning.

Yet I will bide
The ebbing tide
And smile away the sadness,
And at each stroke
Be softly spoke
And calmly await the gladness.

For by my hand
This naked man
I will reflesh and nourish,
And from within
The hidden bin,
Fruits of my gift shall flourish.

John Newlin

The Triumph

Eternal silence is to each
bequeathed, and not by any yet escaped
and that mystery beyond the breath
is mist enshrouded, in Stygian darkness draped,

We do not, dare not, must not know
its meaning, nor whether it be obscene,
nor if it swell ripe with pleasure
melting mortal agony by its scheme.

The traveler departs the inconstant world
wherein never in truth could he say:
"Here have I lived and here I knew glory, "
with expiring breath on his final day.

If man be beset with the cruel rigor
of plague and tempest and carnage of war,
should he not embark the journey gladly,
his arid pain relieved, the tragedy o'er?

But man, the dupe of the solemn comedy
loses his gift in sleep and sterile toil,
no time for visions of the eternal stars,
no great songs snatched from life's bitter coil.

His sons lie broken--crushed in battle's jaws,
fire, flood, and pestilence scourge his land,
and yet he shuns the dark alliance
that offers end of pain to his aching gland.

For man loves the sun and mightily detests
the pale silver dagger that congeals the night.
He lives and loves below the senseless stars
and draws elegant meaning from their light.

What that he were sorely wounded deep
and blood foamed, bubbling at each breath,
living yet would he greater endure
than an end to breathing tendered by death.

Yes, this love of life marks man's glory
and his triumph is secure and great,
for he has suffered, has endured the woe
and-~eyes burning in the darkness--defied his fate,

Petty and puny, man warrants no scorn,
from his faith in life and its sweet breath
has sprung love immortal--immortality
that lives beyond the icy grasp of death.

John Newlin

Remembrance

The world was so much ours to win or lose.
fair was the crown unjeweled, sweet its wearing,
sweeter still, the untilled soil of our daring
to seek the truth and in its finding, refuse
to heed the glare that chills warm dark shadow,

Where are you now, brothers who danced gaily?
Dust or flesh, ash or bone, do you remember
the spring of our youth blooming in September?
And the grounds strewn with leaves rending frailly
like slender gold fronds of El Dorado?

Can you recall from time's mist, repairing
to the tavern, arm by arm, no thought ever
for death, sorrow or life's harsh endeavor?
But our lips kissed the grape, hardly caring,
while in song our voices rang with bravado.

Oh my friends, the maids were fair and callow,
ripe torsos trim and firm--young breasts jutting,
tresses gold and ebon--long legs strutting.
Breeze-soft, like a sigh, their love blew fallow,
stirring our hearts to a fevered staccato.

Laughter, dearer than love's zeal, rang loudly
as we trod youth's fruited plain of yesteryear.
We all, as one, reaped the joy and buried fear
and prayed to scale the stars, vying proudly,
but unknown, the truth lay incommunicado.

Time swallowed up our dreams, quelled our joys.
where are you now, dear comrades of yon day?
I can hear your hearts beating, as if to say:
Come fill the cup again, once more be boys
and dwell in the womb of youth's warm dark
shadow.

John Newlin

Freedom's Song

I would sing my freedom's song
if I possessed the vibrant voice,
sweet tenor or raw baritone,
that would elevate me to choice
between the now and the when,
of the never and the again.

I would build an arch of triumph
would that I owned a stronger hand
with a young grip not yet defunct
to obey the urgent command
to cut the stone and deftly shape
the portal to my escape.

I would ascend into blue heaven
had I again my wings of old,
to wheel and cavort unthreatened
above the misery untold
by one heart's scarred, selfish vision--
the architect of my prison.

She Lays Dying

She lays dying, dying--bathed in pale light,
far the flame gaily burning--out of sight.
her lips cool pallid, limp from foggy breath,
no more ripe halo of scarlet wealth,

Urgent her suffering, soon the hooding down
of cloudy eyes, misted by sorrow's crown.
Her bosom trembles, heaves a metal sigh,
from her loins gone desire, ravished and dry.

Dear her body's lust, dreadful its flying,
limpid her body's flesh, harsh its dying.
Frozen in the grasp of love's glacial pain,
her ruby drum falters in withering bane,

Keen was his dart, subtle its vicious barb,
faithless her archer, clad in lover's garb.
Impaled upon his pitiless arrow,
she fed unbridled thirst out her marrow.

Her flame burned intensely and in its glow
he basked and warmed and fed it fuel to grow,
until the heat baked her honor to dust,
charred and seared into ashes all her lust.

She lays dying, dying--bathed in pale light,
near the flame burning--terrible to see.
Her lips sealed cold now, no more labored breath,
The drum silent--stilled by inconstancy.

John Newlin

The Ship

The ship was blessed as it embarked
upon lifelong voyage o'er the sea
and scripted vows were uttered then
by each the crew of constancy,

A worthy ship and masted tall,
that caught the wind in billowed sail,
responded smartly to the helm
and sliced smooth through foam crested swell.

And summer calm reigned fair and sweet
bading warm breeze to briskly cause
swift, straight passage across the main,
crew unmindful of nature's laws.

A sudden storm then rent the sky,
launching a fiery fateful spear
and tempest's wrathful judgment blind
denied bold captain's vested years.

The vessel heeled and groaned aloud
but soon righted under taut wheel.
"Sail on, sail on!" urged insouciant crew
scorning clear sign of damaged keel.

On they sailed, captain grim and lame,
but not so bent as not to see
that crooked ship and blinded crew
would sail them to despondency.

With winter's gale in summer's stead,
the sea turned angry on the ship,
tossed and whipped her from given course
while bitter rain loosed the captain's grip.

The captain sensed that dead ahead
lurked shallow danger, rocky teeth,
but stayed his hand and held the way
to end the voyage on jaded reef.

Wormy planking and twisted keel
splintered asunder--sharp abort.
tall masted schooner sank below,
leagues and years from intended port.

The captain found himself ashore--
and later, where sea and sand blend,
silently to himself did vow:
never is the day I sail again.

John Newlin

The Riddle

A golden gateway stood alone
out on a distant barren plain,
the shadow of its daunting arch
draped east and west with darkling mane.

Wandering weary, sore of foot,
along a road to me unknown,
I came suddenly beneath it
and heard its massive silence groan.

From whence it came or by whose hand
was a mystery, darkly deep;
its grandeur was no less awesome
than the fear haunting my heart's keep.

Far aloft upon the gilded crest,
nearly too distant from my sight,
was carved the gateway's name: "Moment",
emblazoned bold in stark sky light.

An inner voice within me spoke,
"Behold this moment of now's time.
two long paths underneath it meet,
one to tomorrow, one from prime.

Behind you lies eternity,
ahead all that is yet to come.
the paradox is found between -
the riddle too profound to plumb."

I moved with leaden step ahead.
the voice within me spoke no more
and as I left the golden arch,
I sensed I'd trod this way before.

Long labored hours melted away
before I paused to think and doubt.
Had the gateway been there before?
Would all return yet round about?

John Newlin

She Sleeps Alone

She sleeps alone beside me,
her body a pale silver ghost
of the vivacious siren who
pledged to love and trust me most,

Her slumber echoes in the dark,
across the void that divides us;
short sullen breaths of denial,
gift wrapped in coats of rust.

The room, the bed, the darkness
were hers to keep and never share,
why then did she come the distance
to find and lure me trembling there?

I cast the die - embraced my fate.
love was the prize well worth the risk,
and I, tumbling like that fated die,
went blindly to her fine-spun nest.

Swifter than it had grown, love died,
coldly slain by her other self;
a darker side not sooner shown
submerged me in pain's cruel gulf.

She sleeps alone beside me
dreaming fitfully of the dawn;
when the anguish of her betrayal
injures too much--and I am gone.

The Canyon

A gentle woman took my hand
and led me to the canyon's gate;
the gateway to the old ones' land,
ancient beauty to celebrate.

Her canyon's walls, sheer rock and cliff,
flanked a stony serpentine trail,
in raw sienna splendor, sun's gift;
old ones' cathedral--hers as well.

Sacred visages--solemn, wise--
jut sharply from the ancient walls,
spirits gazing with sightless eyes
like statuesque kachina dolls.

A soaring hawk on silent wing
stalking prey from the turquoise sky,
shed random feather fluttering
to her soft hand, then pressed to mine.

She lead me through the old ones' hall
to a zephyred mesa high above
and bade me lay in a piney mall
to share the sacraments of love.

The Last of the Wine

When the last of the wine
has been poured, red and dry,
and the golden wings of eagles,
burnished by time, dismount the sky.

When the velvet hush of eventide
conquers the ebbing splendor of day
and quick deep laughter, like hope
unraveled, is wilted by time's decay.

Her soft dark eyes will remind me
of love's fragments gathered in bloom;
a bouquet of passion's blossoms
fragrantly spun on love's loom.

And the silent desperate waiting
to swallow up her honeyed breath
will dwell in memory's corridor
until the ardor yields to death.

Stolen hours, like grains of sand,
have been scattered through the years,
venerated by the pain and glory
of our intimacy--and our tears.

The fervent rhythm of her body
has engulfed me in its tide,
interring my dread of failure
where other restive fears reside.

Tasting her where she loves me,
milking the kisses from her lips,
has infused my soul with purpose
and inspired lyric fingertips.

When the sweet magic is ended
and night bird wings mount the sky,
our adventure will have the flavor
of aging wine, red and dry.

By the Sea

Once by the sea I knew her
more than by name
and quicksilver reveries,
more by elusive beauty,
shimmering in the swale
of shapeless time.

Her grace, her poise once etched
in crystallized tears
are veiled and blurred
beyond the watery leagues
of a distance too far.

At night by the sea I search
the invisible horizons
for fragments of yesterday's warmth
to find only the cold ashes
of old devotions.

By the sea, I welcome sleep
to come and whisper
of her to me,
but sleep touches my brow
and speaks not.

The Devil's Maid

The fragrant roses dare not dwell
around the fetid portal of hell
nor do gently and brightly twine
the scarlet leaves of the columbine.

Gone is the beauty time betrayed
that once adorned the Devil's maid.
Dim is the fire that she has banked
deep in love's kiln, now cold and dank.

No crystal drops bedeck her eyes,
wrinkled flesh now line her thighs.
Tis the eleventh hour of life's day,
or if you listen, so she will say.

The Devil's maid has lost her trust
and dotes on wear and age and rust.
Her thoughts are neither clean nor clear,
her image blurs in the Devil's mirror.

Instead of tresses, fine and gold,
she combs his poison through her soul.
Youth is beauty, the Devil said,
when it flees, ash shall crown your head.

And so his silken words she heeds
and dons a garland of his weeds
and sits her down to mourn and pine
for the blessed days of the columbine.

John Newlin

Images

Searing cold vibrations
ringing in the well;
shifting sands in the moonlight
obscuring the only trail.

A song sinking, shattered
upon a dissonant reef;
pregnant clouds low flying
over the tidal grief.

Voices in crescendo
of sharply focused gall;
severed strands fraying
in the fabric of the soul.

Frail wings in the darkness
fleeing a ruptured storm;
footprints in the stardust,
leagues away from home.

Pale cheeks in black boxes
hewed from fated pine;
black lace and white candles
sputtering in the rain.

Reckless thirst rippling
placid pools of bliss;
a rusty mirror reflecting
faint imprint of a kiss.

Fragrant guile oozing
down a fickle brow;
faithless eyes drowning
in the melting of the snow.

Wormy bark peeling on
bent sapling in the glen;
a crown of weighty branches
bowing to the wind.

Such are the graying images
painful in the grasp;
kaleidoscopic fragments
of life's fragile glass,

embedded in the depths
of memory's own thick balm
congealing in the ashes
of a time long since gone.

A Lover's Lie (with apologies to Raleigh)

You have forsaken
this wounded lover
and 'neath silence's veil waste no reply.
But you know certain
sweet words unspoken
in your heart that give your silence the lie.

In your warm bed
you did know me
and with damp eyes shining bade me not fly;
yet with your ardor
banked and cooling,
you deny me, giving your bed the lie.

By your own hand
the wound is given,
with such words my complaint you would deny;
but your silence
is the cruel blade
rending my heart, giving your words the lie.

Bread has been broken
between you and I,
sweet passion's fruit shared with lustful sigh,
and dry, red wine
has passed our lips,
spurring our fervor, giving doubt the lie.

Yet your silence
remains unbroken,
and I know that you will never say why.
But I know your secret,
the fear it holds--
you deny your love, giving it the lie.

Why Music

Why music do I thus fondly embrace
in lieu of bending to the planet's din
or knowing an atom's relative place
and the search for the mysteries therein?

Why do l spurn the fog of fluid grain
and turn hard away from the tainted leaf,
preferring rather a plaintive refrain
embodied in a tenor's dulcet grief?

Is it in the need so to emulate
the hue and passion of musical tone
and thus by my heart's rhythm orchestrate
the kneeling close by sweet melody's throne?

The liquid beauty of harmonic chord
fills my cup brimming with its sweet reward.

Now That He Is Gone

Sleep, exhausted mistress,
now that he is gone,
love's memory will warm you
when your dreams are done.

Embrace the dawn's melting
into a newborn day,
rise with refreshed body
now he has gone his way.

Tempt only empty shadows
with your charm and glow,
your lover cannot love you
nor burn your candle low.

Sweet repose awaits you,
when to your bed you creep,
there his essence lingers
to join you in your sleep.

There Was a Time

There was a time when
the world seemed sweetly frozen,
only moving in halting, dreamy frames,
and the silhouettes of tomorrow
barely revealed our names.

There was a year when
the winds teased our restless sails
with a laughing zephyr breeze
and our course but briefly traced
its artless wake in the seas.

There was a season when
summer's forge heated and fused
the clarity of our combined vision
into an alloy of timeless joy
and the passion of ambition.

There was a day when
our heart's fitful, fated beating
obscured the delicate reality
of the tempo of our journey
to our encounter with mortality.

The time, the year, the season,
and the day have passed and gone.
The recognition of journey's end
now intones the lamentation
for that which might have been.

Alas Dear Madam

Alas dear Madam, have I wronged you
by gesture, unkind word, or deed,
thus giving you cause for sorrow
importuning your heart to bleed?

Have I, dear Madam, given you
injury so rank and so low
as to merit your cool design
to suffer me the status quo?

Dear Madam, have I deceived you
and showered you with silken lies,
or primed you with honeyed words
to cloak dark purpose in disguise?

No, dear Madam, no wrong to you
did I meanly perpetrate.
No grievous sin did I commit,
nor insult coldly dedicate.

My grossest error, dear Madam,
was to insensibley explore
the pride steeping in your bosom
and its delicacy ignore.

So dear Madam, please forgive me
for numb bruises I numbly gave
to that one part of a woman
which no man should ever brave.

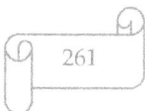

John Newlin

Afterglow

I loved her from afar,
from a distance
measured in miles,
seasons and years,
delusions and fears,
verses and tears.

I loved an image,
a shadow of her,
a moonbeam in my hand,
no form to touch,
no hand to clutch,
nor embrace's rush.

I loved a memory,
kept warm and alive
from day to night,
to invade my sleep,
in dreams to creep,
raiding my soul's keep.

Then she lay
at my side,
and I have held her
breathless and near,
so close and dear,
a heart to revere.

How could I ever let
her slip away again,
after all these years,
now that again I know
passion's peak and flow
into love's sweet afterglow.

John Newlin

Requiem For A Fallen Warrior

After each empty year
we shall solemnly return
to the lea, your stone.

Where strong oaks and tall birch,
stand reverently on guard
over your earthly peace.

Bouquets of colored blossoms
infuse the cool still air
with their hallowed fragrance.

A tear or two, perhaps more
shall be shed for the loss
of your sturdy presence.

But also knowing smiles
for the glad times,
before the day you fell.

There is no war here,
in this tranquil glade;
only reflective harmony.

There is no sand here,
no coarse grains of Babylon
steeped in your blood.

You stand at ease in our hearts
where you whisper secrets
of love's timeless grace.

You shall be remembered,
not just when we stand near
but every day of our lives.

"Day is done, gone the sun.."

John Newlin

The Old One

The old one reached down
into the cellar of his remembrance
and found a faded image
of a paramour;
a love lost so long ago.

He burnished it
and restored its lustrous glow,
and in his heart's forge
shaped a silver frame
to hold the beauty
untarnished by time.

Index

A

A Gem, 154
A Glass of Wine, 36
A Lover's Lie, 256
A Mother's Lament, 172
A Mother's Goodbye, 107
A New Day, 180
A Poem, 207
A Poem Not Written, 165
A Poet's Fate, 7
A Question, 216
A Sadder Man, 111
A Spinster, 170
A Sweet Gig, 82
A Whisper, 187
Afterglow, 262
Alas Dear Madam, 229, 261
Alone, 167
Ambivalence, 58
An Unwritten Poem, 44
Another Day, 123
Another Dream, 209
Artists, 8
Autumn Heart, 126

B

Babylon's Fields, 67
Babylon's Honor, 88
Best Friend, 97
Beyond the Pale, 1
By the Sea, 252

C

Cassius Crow, 200
Christine, 7
Christmas Day, 39
Climb a Tree, 51
Coffee, 168
Cold Memory, 52
Collapse the Night, 19

Colors, 50
Come Back Moses, 221
Consensual Sax, 93
Could I But Know, 236
Cyber Poetry, 25

D

Death's Claim, 228
Demon Dream, 132
Despair, 143
Dignity, 103
Discovery, 189
Distant Affections, 13
Dreams, 153
Dust, 131

E

Epiphany, 120
Evening in Babylon, 86

F

Faith and Fear, 20
Fallen Statues, 76
Fear, 188
Firestorm, 128
Footprints, 136
For Alisha, 61
Foregiveness, 27
Freedom's Song, 242
Friend and Foe, 140
Friendship, 157
Friendship And Wine, 188

G

Garden of Love, 164
Gethsemane, 46
Girl Underwater, 118
Glass Heart, 137
Goodbyes, 156

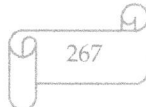

H

Harsh Words, 138
Helen, 226
Her Memory, 160
Her Shoppe, 121
Her Silence, 235
Her Voices, 182
How Could She Not, 129
How To Die, 122
Humanus Mathematica, 134

I

I Am a Ship, 106
I Could Forget, 166
I lost Her, 85
If Love Is To Be, 195
Images, 254
Ivory and Ebony (for George Shearing), 31

J

Judith Anne, 2

L

L' Auberge, 110
Lady of the Night, 73
Last Notes, 28
Life, 56
Life and Limb, 77
Life's Debris, 71
Love and He, 202
Love's Labor, 215
Love's Wheel, 42

M

Marionette, 152
Maybe, 144
Memories, 26, 115, 190
My Father, 210
Mystery, 176
Mystery of the Horn, 92

N

Night Launch, 222
Now That He Is Gone, 259
Numbers, 194

O

Old Friend, 212
On The Beach, 35
Once I Knew Thee, 218
One Night With Venus, 196
Our Days, 48
Our First Christmas, 162
Over There, 66

P

Paper Airplane, 38
Paradox, 10
Pearls, 181

R

Redemption, 175
Regrets, 34
Remembrance, 240
Requiem For A Fallen Warrior, 264
Revenge, 64
Rise and Fall, 43
Risk, 208

S

Satchmo, 74
Saving The Tiger, 192
Schism, 150
Sea of Dreams, 108
Serena From Verbena, 78
She and He, 145
She Lays Dying, 243
She Sleeps Alone, 248
Some Things, 65
Someday, 205
Sometime, 11, 147
Soul Lover, 198

Southeast of April, 232
Sun, Moon, and Stars, 4
Sweet Soul Mate, 206

T

Tennessee Valley, 63
Thanksgiving, 164
That Night, 59
The Arabesque, 101
The Asylum, 96
The Belle, 99
The Bereaved, 72
The Canyon, 249
The Challenge, 16
The Colorist, 55
The Crystal Spider, 177
The Dance, 121
The Day, 214
The Devil's Maid, 253
The Dilemma, 184
The Distance, 158
The Drifter, 220
The Drowning, 30
The Essence, 149
The Glass, 54, 70
The Going, 94
The Good Life, 90
The Insult, 32
The Last of the Wine, 250
The Last Soul Mate, 146
The Look of Her, 174
The Metaphor, 9
The Moon, 112
The Mystery, 33
The Old One, 266
The Old Tiger, 204
The Poem I Wish She Had Written, 163
The Poet's Conundrum, 37
The Poet's Gift, 199
The Poet's Table, 24
The Precipice, 22
The Prism, 114
The Recipe, 130
The Resurrection, 234

The Reverie, 113
The Riddle, 246
The River, 230
The Road, 139
The Rose, 98
The Sax Man, 80
The Scent of Darkness, 57
The Sea, 224
The Ship, 244
The Stone Garden, 47
The Triumph, 238
The Two, 119
The Walk, 148
The Way of Dreams, 109
Then She Was Gone, 60
There Was a Time, 260
They, 40
Things Unsaid, 171
Thy Beauty, 219
Tightrope, 178
Time, 169
Time Warp, 62
To Forget, 161
To Tell A Love, 217
Today & Tomorrow, 102
Too Much, 17
Treasures, 29, 155
Two Hearts, 191
Two Ships, 16

U

Upland Promise, 124

V

Vacancy, 100
Verse, 49
Vertigo, 18
Voices, 225

W

Wallflower, 99
We Danced, 12
We Leap, 14

John Newlin

What If?, 68
Why Music, 258
Winter Heart, 116
Winter Pain, 23

Y

Years, 151
You Are a Poet, 104

About the Author

John Newlin grew up in Springfield, Illinois where he attended grade school and high school before attending Illinois College in Jacksonville, Illinois. Even though he loved the small college environment he realized he had no viable career plan so he left college in the middle of his junior year to work for the State of Illinois in a concrete testing lab while he considered his career options.

John always wanted to fly, so he applied to the Navy for acceptance in the Naval Aviation Cadet program. His application was accepted and he was inducted as a Cadet in July of 1957 at the Naval Air Station St. Louis, Missouri. His father died during his transit from St. Louis to Pensacola thus his first two weeks on active duty were spent on emergency leave.

Following his father's funeral, John returned to NAS Pensacola to begin his flight training. He was designated a Naval Aviator and commissioned an Ensign in May of 1959. During his 23 year career in the Navy, he flew fighter jets from the decks of 11 different aircraft carriers in the Pacific and Atlantic Oceans and the Mediterranean Sea. He saw aerial combat in the skies over North Vietnam in the summer of 1967. John was serving aboard U.S.S. Forrestal and U.S.S. Enterprise when both suffered horrendous flight deck fires.

John applied for and was selected to participate in the Navy's College Degree Program to allow former Naval Aviation Cadets to earn a baccalaureate degree in one calendar year. He earned a Bachelor of Arts degree in mathematics at San Diego State University in the summer of 1970.

After his retirement from the Navy in February of 1980, John worked as a systems analyst and software engineer for several San Diego based Department of Defense contractors, including Computer Sciences Corporation and Hughes Aircraft. While working for Computer Sciences Corporation he earned a Bachelor of Science degree in Computer Science. John left Hughes in 1987 to market personal computer software that he had developed. He operated his software business for 11 years before retiring to Vista, California. During 1987 and 1988 John was a regular contributor of technical articles to The Programmer's Journal magazine.

John's best friend is his wonderful sister Carol Armstrong, who lives in Overgaard, Arizona. His lovely daughter Deidre, is a psychologist living in Oceanside, California. His most favorite nieces are

Janet Schomaker of Mesa, Arizona and Sandy Love of Salida, California.

John wrote his first poem in his stateroom aboard U.S.S. Ranger at sea in 1974 and has been writing ever since. A former friend and soul mate, Judith Anne Hewson, was the inspiration for many of the poems in this collection for which he is most grateful. John's favorite poets are JB Stillwater, Katriona Wallace, Sylvia Plath, Emily Dickinson, and Pablo Neruda.

www.ingramcontent.com/pod-product-compliance
Lightning Source LLC
Chambersburg PA
CBHW071654090426
42738CB00009B/1517